THE EMPIRICAL AND ADVANCED KNOWLEDGE OF JESUS AND THE REAL COMMONWEALTH OF ISRAEL

THE EMPIRICAL AND ADVANCED KNOWLEDGE OF JESUS AND THE REAL COMMONWEALTH OF ISRAEL

DAVID EBUBE ISRAEL

Re-Published in the **(USA)** by: 2 Covenant Mogul Publishing House LLC

Dr. Serena Washington, is the Owner of 2 Covenant Mogul Publishing House

Website:www.pcspublishinguniversity.com

DEDICATION

This book is dedicated to our Father the Majesty in heaven, to the Lord Jesus Christ our Great High Priest after the order of Melchizedek, to the Lamb's blood on the Cross-, to the Comforter even the Holy Ghost and Power of the Highest and to all His saints on earth.

ACKNOWLEDGEMENTS

I acknowledge all the saints who have been praying for us and for the prosperity of God's work in our hands. May the grace of our Lord Jesus, the love of God and the communion of the Holy Spirit be with you.

TABLE OF CONTENTS

Chapter 1	**Resolving the well-known challenge of all time>>>>>**	12
Chapter 2	My strange encounter>>>>>>>>>>>>>>>>>>>>>>>>>>	16
Chapter 3	Demystifying the mystery>>>>>>>>>>>>>>>>>>>>>>>	20
Chapter 4	The best prayer for Orthodox Jews>>>>>>>>>>>>>>>	28
Chapter 5	Jesus revealed in the book of Psalms >>>>>>>>>>>>>	33
Chapter 6	Waiters on the Lord >>>>>>>>>>>>>>>>>>>>>>>>>>>	39
Chapter 7	Jesus Coded In the Book of Isaiah>>>>>>>>>> >>>>>>	48
Chapter 8	Jesus and Zaccheus>>>>>>>>>>>>>>>>>>>>>>>>>>>>>	56
Chapter 9	The Watch Tower Society (Jehovah's Witness) and Jesus>>>>>>>>>>>>>>>>>>>>>>>>>>>>>>>>>>>>>	72
Chapter 10	Understanding the Mystery of the Aleph–Tau in Psalm 119>>>>>>>>>>>>>>>>>>>>>>>>>>>>>>>>>>>	87
Chapter 11	The Patriarchal–Sequential Order from Adam to Israel In Connection with the Aleph-Tau>>>>>>>>>>>>>>>>	107
Chapter 12	Errors and Conspiracy of the Roman Catholic Church>>>>>>>>>>>>>>>>>>>>>>>>>>>>>>>>>>>>	115
Chapter 13	The Real Commonwealth of Israel As Written & Reported By Apostle Paul>>>>>>>>>>>>>>>>>>>>>>>	126
Chapter 14	Prayer of Deliverance from Sins (Demons)>>>>>>>	132
Chapter 15	The Salvation of the people of Israel >>>>>>>>> >>>	137

FOREWORD

This book is a timely message to the Jews and Gentiles across the world that are looking forward to the arrival of the *'SALVATION and HOPE'* of Israel. It is a workbook to those with a divine mandate to minister to the Jews, Islam and the whole world.
It is a stone among others, that fixes the desolate places, that restores foundations of many generations, that builds a bridge in the breach that exists between the Jews and the new covenant church that restores the paths.

Brother David, as a master builder, has skillfully laid a solid stone on the foundation that Christ laid, upon which all His saints build a holy habitation and a dwelling place for the Lord. I recommend this book to all who hope for Israel and the world at large to be saved and those who want to return to the shepherd of their souls and their national treasure.

Elder Nathaniel Ndukwe
Missionary

As we are part of an ever changing global society, it is theologically imperative to reflect on the equivocal paradigms lingering in the minds of both believers and non- believers. It is this mammoth task; the book tries to help us with.

The author leads the readers through the process of theological interpretation and reflections that are conceptually concise and applicable. It gives an in depth knowledge of who Jesus the Christ was in the Old Testament in correlation to testimonies and perfect interpretations in relevant references. The book emphasizes the author's points in every chapter with accurate tables to match, carving it as a master class of inspirational excellence... A Must Read.

Allan Gee

INTRODUCTION

In every society and among mature minds, inquisitiveness is the mark of a devoted scholar. Inquisitiveness is akin to a pebble gone in search of the bottomless deep. That pebble passes through several layers of the deep sea until it reaches and settles down in the bottom of the sea. Since man is created with inquisitive instincts, the Creator of man has also provided accurate and perfect answers to every question that may arise from man, whether it is about the creation itself or the Creator Himself. Since all the religions in the world are either pro–Christ or anti–Christ in practice, there is need for us to provide a comprehensive, an empirical and an advanced knowledge of the encoded name of 'Jesus' of Nazareth in the Old Testament in dealing with any curiosity in the minds of men and women. The Bible has provided suitable answers to every question that may arise from any religion of the world about the person of 'Jesus.' Resolving the most well-known challenge of all time is the primary focus of this book. This most heated up and debated well-known challenge of all time is "Where Can We Find the Name "Jesus" In the Old Testament?" This mountainous challenge has posed many difficulties to the faith of many people in the world today especially among the Orthodox and unbelieving Jews.

The Islamic world is also very curious to know where in the Bible our Lord Jesus referred to Himself as "God." In order to convert Orthodox Jews from Judaism to Jesus Christ and turn the curious Islamic world and other religions to the blessed Son of God—Jesus of Nazareth, we must provide ample and soothing answers to their questions by resolving them Biblically. Please understand the burning heartbeat of the very God that loves the world for all men, all races and the entire world; "Who will have all men to be saved and come to the knowledge of the truth" (1 Timothy 2:4).

Getting men saved through evangelism is part of God's heartbeat but bringing all men and all races to the knowledge of the truth is the utmost goal and heartbeat of our God. Therefore, we can say that the gospel of the Kingdom of heaven is divided into two sections and these are:

- ❖ Having all men saved and all men coming to the knowledge of the truth.

THE TWO CATEGORIES OF PEOPLE ON EARTH

There are two categories of people on earth and they are:

- The wise and prudent
- Unassuming babies who desire the sincere milk of the Word.

God actually wants to reveal Himself to humankind but He only does so to babes and unassuming ones. However, He normally hides Himself from the wise and prudent. "At that time Jesus answered and said, I thank thee, O Father, Lord of heaven and earth, because thou hast hid these things from the wise and prudent, and hast revealed them unto babes. Even so, Father: for so it seemed good in thy sight. All things are delivered unto me of my Father: and no man knoweth the Son, but the Father; neither knoweth any man the Father, save the Son, and he to whomsoever the Son will reveal him" (Matthew 11:25-27).

The mystery behind the knowledge of our Lord Jesus depends solely on the Father's revelation of His Son to babes and suckling only. Our heavenly Father does not reveal and trust the mysteries of His Son Jesus Christ to the wise and prudent men of this world. If we are wise and prudent according to the standard of this world instead of being babes in God's sight, His Holy Spirit will always hide the mysteries of Jesus from us. The Father, the Son and the Holy Spirit only walk with babes who hunger and thirst for the pure knowledge of His Son as revealed and written in the Scriptures of Truth.

When Paul was converted from Judaism and the tradition of his fathers' religion to the Lord Jesus the Christ, his hunger and quest were for him to know Jesus and the power of His resurrection. "But what things were gain to me, those I counted loss for Christ. Yea doubtless, and I count all things but loss for the Excellency of the knowledge of Christ Jesus my Lord: for whom I have suffered loss of all things, and do count them but dung, that I may win Christ. And be found in him, not having my own righteousness, which is of the law, but that which is through the faith of Christ, the righteousness which is of God by faith: That I may know him, and the power of his resurrection, and the fellowship of his sufferings, being made conformable unto his death" (Philippians 3:7-10).

Our brother being a Hebrew and a Jew knew and studied in their school of Judaism about the “Salvation of Israel” who is also called the 'Hope' of Israel and their fathers. Paul who studied under, Gamaliel, the great doctor and teacher of the Jewish law knew, spoke, wrote and taught Hebrew language. Having been through with his study of the Jewish law based on the Tanakh (Old Testament) Genesis to Malachi, he was familiar with the prophecy of Israel their father in Genesis 49:18, which states, “I have waited for your salvation, O LORD.”

The Hebrew word for “Salvation” is “Yeshua” (Jesus) and the Hebrew word for the Messiah is Mashiach (Christ).” In the Hebrew curriculum of studies based on the Scriptures of the prophets, the knowledge of the “Salvation of Israel” was their primary, secondary and tertiary studies. They were ardent students and exponents of the prophecies of their patriarchal fathers namely Abraham, Isaac, Israel and other prophets who pointed their nation to the 'Salvation' that is to come. The two main central focuses in their traditional Hebraic/Jewish curriculum were (a) 'the Salvation of Israel' (Genesis 49:18), and (b) 'Messiah the Prince' (Psalm 2:110, Psalm 72:1-end and Daniel 9:25).

When The Holy Ghost converted our brother Paul from Judaism to the Lord Jesus the Christ, he (Paul) went into further research of the Tanakh (Old Testament) to know more about the 'Salvation of Israel.' This is because our Lord Jesus said we should search the Scriptures for they testify about Him. In Paul's advanced studies, he made some astonishing discoveries. “Wherefore henceforth know we no man after the flesh: yea, though we have known Christ after the flesh, yet now henceforth know we him no more.” (2 Corinthians 5:16). He realized that the Man called Jesus of Nazareth was not just a New Testament hero or an initiator– series–person.

Through detailed perceptual study of the Scriptures, Brother Paul understood that Jesus of Nazareth was the very ancient “Salvation of Israel” that he, their fathers and others had studied, talked about and waited for. When Apostle Paul got the revelation of the “Salvation of Israel” who is called “Jesu” or “Jesus” by the Greco-Roman world and “Yeshua” or “Yahshua” by the Jewish people, he counted all the things he had acquired as dung because of the Excellency of the knowledge of Christ Jesus our Lord. For the Father to speak to and teach us the hidden mysteries of Jesus Christ coded in all the books of Genesis to Malachi and made crystal clear from the books of Matthew to Revelation by His Spirit, we must be converted from being wise and prudent men to babes and unassuming persons.

The wealth of the excellent knowledge of Jesus Christ that Paul had was released to him, as he became a babe in the Father's sight.

The purpose of this book is to provide a comprehensive, an advanced insight and knowledge of the Person of the 'Salvation of Israel' for our generation and other succeeding generations who will be great exponents of the Lord Jesus and His name in all the nations of the world as the Scriptures have revealed. This book is a guide to deeper insights, higher and advanced applications of the knowledge of Christ. Apostle Paul and other apostles also discovered that our Lord Jesus Christ is the very 'Commonwealth of Israel.' This awesome discovery became part of the driving divine force that helped them to evangelize the nations into being members of the "Commonwealth of Israel."

A Common wealth is defined as what a league of nations or a people share in common as their greatest treasures or resources, which every member enjoys mutually whether poor or rich, educated or illiterate, wise or foolish. An example is the Commonwealth of Nations of the old British Empire.

Paul's revelation of the 'Commonwealth of Israel', which states that the Gentiles are to become partakers in Christ Jesus, is the Holy Spirit's seal of Sonship. Ephesians 1:13-14 describes the seal of the Holy Spirit on those who believe as "the earnest of their inheritance." The Holy Spirit is the very Spirit of Christ. If He is our earnest inheritance, then, He is our most treasured wealth that does not perish. The kings and prophets of Israel enjoyed this wealth privilege for thousands of years until the Holy Ghost was poured out upon all flesh as prophesied by the prophet, Joel. Therefore, as long as the Spirit of Christ was upon the sons of Israel in their ranks, they prospered above all nations.

Members of the 'Commonwealth of Israel' are privileged to be partakers of the Holy Spirit who is in Christ without any dichotomy. Nevertheless, do the Orthodox Jews recognize that their "Commonwealth" is Jesus of Nazareth the Christ? This is where this book deals with the plan of God to bring the Jews and the Gentile believers to recognize their eternal source of wealth or the 'Commonwealth' that unites the Jews and Gentiles and begin to appreciate their inheritance.

CHAPTER 1

RESOLVING THE WELL-KNOWN CHALLENGE OF ALL TIME ...

For many centuries, there has been a well-known challenge among the Jews in Europe, America, and Asia and in other parts of the world. This challenge has led to the denial of the faith by so many people in the world.

In this book, we are going to deal with this particular well-known challenge in details from the books of Genesis to Malachi and from the gospels of Matthew to John. One day, a friend of ours who travelled to London in the year 2013, called my wife and I and told us that she had an issue with her niece. Her niece has been a Christian for a long time but at the time, she started attending lectures on Judaism and other religions. She said that her niece told her that there is no place, where the name **"JESUS"** can be found in the Old Testament. She implied that the Old Testament prophets from Genesis to Malachi did not write anything about **JESUS** in their prophecies and as a result of this, she does not believe any longer in the 'Person and Name' of the Lord **JESUS** found in the New Testament from the books of Matthew to Revelation.

This most heated debate—***"You can't find Jesus"*** in the Old Testament has been a well-known challenge in the past one thousand eight hundred years. In places like U.K, U.S.A, Scotland, Germany, and many parts of Europe, Africa, Asia, etc. where Judaism thrives with vigour, this has been the mainstream reason why so many people do not embrace the Lord Jesus of Nazareth the true Messiah/Christ of the Jews and the world.

The most adept question that stirs our face is this, "Where can we find the name **"JESUS"** in the Old Testament/Hebrew Scriptures?"

Arthur Glass shares his experience with us. He said and I quote him, "In dealing with my Jewish brethren for many years in Canada, the United States, Argentina and Uruguay, I had one difficulty. It was this: *My Jewish people would always fling at me this challenging question, 'If Jesus is our Messiah and the whole Old Testament is about Him, how come His name is never mentioned in it even once?'* " Mr. Arthur Glass said that he could not answer it satisfactorily to their way of thinking and he admitted that he often wondered why Jesus' name was not actually written in the Old Testament Bible. He said that he could show them His divine titles in Isaiah 7:14, 9:6 and Jeremiah 23:5-6 and even the word "Messiah" in several places, but the Hebrew name that would be equal to **"JESUS"** that he could not show."

So, this very challenge has been an issue that needs to be resolved biblically. All the Jews know that the name **"Messiah"** appears in the Bible as it was revealed to Daniel. *"Know therefore and understand that from the going forth of the commandment to restore and to rebuild Jerusalem unto Messiah the Prince shall be seven weeks and threescore and two weeks the street shall be built again and the wall even in troublous times. And after threescore and two weeks shall Messiah be cut off, but not for himself"* (Daniel9:24-25). Nevertheless, the challenging question is where in the Old Testament Bible from the book of Genesis to Malachi can we find the name **"JESUS?"** Did He actually preexist as some people claim and teach or did He just emerge from the New Testament series?

It is because of this issue that most Orthodox Jews do not believe in the New Testament Bible. To this effect, we are admonished to provide satisfactory answers to those who dare ask us questions about the assurance of our faith in **JESUS**, *"But sanctify the Lord God in your hearts and be ready always to give an answer to every man that asketh you a reason of the hope that is in you with meekness and fear"* (1Peter 3:15).

As children of God, the Holy Spirit wants us to provide answers to every bothering question on the Person of our **"Lord Jesus"** who is the hope of glory in us. However, for us to do this, we must review the words that Apostle Paul wrote to Evangelist Timothy bearing on studying for approval, *"Study to show yourself approved unto God, a workman that needeth not to be ashamed, rightly dividing the word of truth"* (2 Timothy 2:15).

For us to provide satisfactory and wholesome answers to this challenging puzzle that stares us on our faces as to where the name **"JESUS"** can be found in the Old Testament, we must commit ourselves to studying the **Word of God** so that we can show ourselves approved unto God. It is only through a devoted study of God's written Word that He can absorb us into being His workers according to His purpose that will not be ashamed or confused, whenever we are confronted with some puzzling and intelligent questions that defy bravery. An Igbo (one of the tribes in Nigeria) native adage says, ***"Intelligence defies bravery but bravery is the test of intelligence."***

In this passage of the book of 2Timothy 2:15, we are not being admonished to ***"pray"*** so as to show ourselves approved unto God but to ***"study."*** This particular issue has become a serious problem among many Christians. Many Christians call themselves prayer warriors and prayer machines, but at a close examination, you will realize that they are not ardent students of God's Word and for this reason; God cannot trust them with greater visions of His Son and His Kingdom.

The primary reason we are still in this world is that we might fix in their proper orders the things that are not yet in place and not for us to ***"church"*** around. *"For this cause I left thee in Crete, that thou shouldest set in order the things that are wanting, and ordain elders in every city, as I had appointed thee"* (Titus1:5).

This very Scripture and the admonition of Apostle Paul to Evangelist Timothy perfectly agree with the Lord's prayer, supplication and intercession for His Church as thus; *"And now I am no more in the world, but* RESOLVING THE WELL KNOWN CHALLENGE OF ALL TIME *these are in the world, and I come to thee. Holy Father, keep through thine own name those that thou hast given me, that they may be one, as we are one. I pray not that thou shouldest take them out of the world, but that thou shouldest keep them from evil"* (John17:11 &15)

Our Lord Jesus Christ who is the ***"centre and focus"*** of the most heated debate in most parts of the world, prayed to His Father that He should not take us out of the world but rather keep us from the evil one. Our primary assignment for being in the world must be re –defined and re-evaluated in order for us to achieve maximum results that will bring shame on the haters of the name and Person of our **Lord Jesus the Christ.**

There are many haters of the name **"JESUS"**, who is the very God and Saviour of the world. All Freemasons, all Islamic world and other religions hate Him with passion, although this is to their detriment. *"Oh that my people had hearkened unto me, and Israel had walked in my ways! I should soon have subdued their enemies, and turned my hands against their adversaries. The haters of God should have submitted themselves unto him: but their time should have endured forever"* (Psalm 81:13-15).

The moment the Lamb's Church begins to hearken to God and walk in His ways through deep Bible study, meditation and practice, those that hate **"JESUS"** will surrender to God. One of the main reasons the Church is left here on earth is for them to teach the principalities and powers in heavenly places the manifold wisdom of God through His written Word. We must provide an institute for advanced study of the Person of our Lord **JESUS *CHRIST*** within the context of the Bible to pull down every high thing that exalts itself against the knowledge of Christ.

CHAPTER 2

MY STRANGE ENCOUNTER

In the month of October 2013 as I was travelling from Lagos to the Eastern part of Nigeria, via Orizu Motors Transport Company, we were about fifteen passengers on board including the driver. As our Christian custom demands, our long or short journeys cannot be complete until prayers are made to God for protection. Therefore, one of the female passengers had just finished leading us in a long session of songs and prayers with the rest of the commuters joining her in praying for journey mercy. Then after the prayers were over, I shared with them the problem our friend faced in the UK and then raised this same question to them with high expectation that at least I would get a good and encouraging response.

However, the reverse was the case. I simply presented this very challenging question of all time to the supposed fellow Christians in a very gentle way as this "Someone said that there is no passage of the Bible from Genesis to Malachi where the name **"JESUS"** is mentioned, what are your views about this highly heated and debated issue? I asked.

As I waited for some Biblical soothing words and answers, I was confronted with some terrible feedbacks from virtually all the commuters that had just finished praying. The entire passengers saw me as an occult man in the midst of born again children of God. Suddenly, the situation in the vehicle changed. They started singing some Christian warfare songs involving Christ's blood and calling down fire from heaven. This scenario lasted for about 35minutes.

I noticed that the driver was a bit afraid. Then I pretended not to be part of them. As the spiritual war songs echoed, I noticed that the woman sitting close to me was closely watching me with shivers. I kept very quiet still. However, I neither sang nor prayed with them because I wanted to see the level of discernment they had. I noticed also that they used prayers as shields. This encounter and experience really opened my eyes the more on the level of ignorance among many Pentecostal and Orthodox Churches who pretend to be praying but their prayers are frenetic in content. In the Church of Jesus Christ, I have noticed a deep-seated level of ignorance in the Bible and this really gives me a great and deep concern.

After a while, I turned to a man by my side and started explaining some issues to him from the Bible. When he noticed that I was not an occult man or anti-Christ fellow, he gave me full attention for Bible discussions. Then, the rest of the passengers appeared as though they were delivered from fear of the unknown. It is because of this experience among my own very fellow Christians and the experiences of other men like Arthur E. Glass that led me into deeper research in the Bible. This book would serve as our contribution in the ***"Tikkun ha'Olam"*** (Repairing of the World) project as revealed in the Bible. *"And they that shall be of thee shall build the old waste places: they shalt raise up the foundations of many generations; and thou shalt be called, The repairer of the breach, The restorer of paths to dwell in"* (Isaiah 58:12).

The Holy Ghost has called us to repair all the breaches and restore all the paths before the second coming of the Lord Jesus Christ the King. In all the nations, people who are studying Judaism have been deceived on this issue about our Lord Jesus. Several high walls have been erected between the Old Testament and the New Testament Bible. These high walls are standing among many Orthodox Jews, Orthodox and Pentecostal Churches, and the people of the world. Our allotted work by our Lord Jesus is for us to depend on the Holy Spirit who alone will help us build a **"bridge"** (instead of a **"wall"**) that connects the Old Testament and New Testament in a perfect and straight-line order and bond.

There are strong mysterious networkings and bonding between the Old Testament and New Testament that only God can reveal to babes and sucklings but not to the wise and prudent.

UNLOCKING OF THE SCRIPTURES

Every chapter and verse of the Bible is under a heavy divine padlock of heaven. The only Person that has the keys to unlock these biblical gates called ***"Chapters"*** and

Biblical doors called ***"verses"*** is the Holy Spirit. The Bible is so awesome and full of mysteries that unless you are a friend of the Holy Spirit, you will only gloss over the chapters and verses of the Bible without plunging into the endless depths of the riches of Christ. *"In that hour Jesus rejoiced in the Spirit, and said, I thank thee, O Father, Lord of heaven and earth, that thou hast hid these things from the wise and prudent, and has revealed them to babes: even so, Father; for so it seemed good in thy sight"* (Luke 10:21).

Our Saviour Jesus the Christ plainly reveals to us that our heavenly Father has hidden His mysteries from the wise and the prudent. He said the Father reveals them unto babes. Therefore, in essence, God finds it much easier and accessible in dealing with babes than He does with the wise and the prudent. Please take note of this; you cannot carry your own wisdom to the palace of King Solomon. Today a man that is greater than Solomon is here. Jesus Christ who is the power and wisdom of God is the Man! We cannot approach Him with our own wisdom. Every form of wisdom and prudence grows pale before Him.

From the book of Genesis to Malachi, the name and the person of ***"JESUS"*** is coded in a way that only those whose eyes have been opened by the Holy Ghost can see it. In this context, we will be looking at what the Jews call 'JESUS,' what the Greeks call 'JESUS,' and what Latin people call *'JESUS'* in their native dialects and languages respectively. This discovery will help us restore the perfect bond of unity between the Old and New Testaments.

This is the age of increased knowledge as God revealed in His word to Daniel as thus, *"But thou, O Daniel, shut up the words, and seal the book, even to the time of the end: many shall run to and fro, and knowledge shall be increased" (Daniel12:4).*

The question is, "Where do we find that Name?" You may ask. Here it is my beloved ones. Every time the Old Testament uses the word ***"Salvation"*** especially with the Hebrew suffix meaning, ***"My" "Thy" or "His" Salvation,*** it means ***"JESUS"*** as we shall see later. In the Hebrew Bible as you read from recto (right) to verso (left), whenever you come across this word: it reads ***"YESHUA" OR "YAHSHUA."***

For further verification of this mystery hidden in the Bible, you may refer to **'THE INTERLINEAR BIBLE'- (**Hebrew, Greek and English). In any verse or passage of the

Hebrew Bible wherever you see... ...it is translated ***Yeshua/Yahshua.*** Then this name ***"Yeshua/Yahshua"*** is translated ***"Salvation"*** in English language as we can see in the Bible. Having established the above truth, let us proceed further on this issue. We are going to base our discovery on the revealed Word of God from angel Gabriel on his visit to Joseph and also on the prayers of Simeon the high priest in the Temple of Jerusalem.

SEE THE TABLE BELOW FOR SPIRITUAL INSIGHT			
Hebrew	**Greek**	**Latin**	**English**
Yeshua	**Iesus/Jesus**	**Iesous/Jesus**	**Salvation**
ישוע= Yeshua = Iesus		**Iesous = Jesus =Salvation**	

In the ancient Hebrew writing this word..., is translated and pronounced **'Yeshua'/'Yahshua'** by the Jews. In Greek **'Yeshua'/'Yahshua"** is translated and pronounced **'Iesus.'** In Latin **'Yeshua/Yahshua'** is translated and pronounced **'Iesous.'** In English language, **'Yeshua'/ 'Yahshua'** is translated as **'Salvation.'** For clearer understanding of the mystery of God coded in every chapter of the Bible, we are going to read it from different translations.

CHAPTER 3

DEMYSTIFYING THE MYSTERY

"And she shall bring forth a son, and thou shall call his name JESUS: for he shall save his people from their sins" (Mathew1:21, KJV)... *"She will give birth to a son, and you are to name him YESHUA (which means Adonai saves) because he will save his people from their sins"* (Mathew1:21, Complete Jewish Bible).

Let us remember that the angel who spoke to Mary physically, is also the same angel who spoke to Joseph in his dream. This angel did not speak in English, Latin or Greek language but in Hebrew language. Again, neither of this couple was slow to grasp the meaning of the significance of the ***"NAME"*** of this divine Son and its relation to its character and His work of redemption. For in the Old Testament all great characters were given names with specific and significant meanings. Since angel Gabriel spoke to Mary and Joseph in Hebrew dialect, he pronounced the name of the Son of the Highest that Mary would bear for God ***"Yeshua/Yahshua."***

THE GOD - GIVEN PRIMARY ASSIGNMENT OF JOHN THE BAPTIST AMONG THE JEWS

"To give knowledge of salvation unto his people by the remission of their sins" (Luke 1:77). The Holy Ghost, who spoke through Zechariah the father of John the Baptist, said that he (John) would give knowledge of ***"Salvation"*** (Yeshua/Jesus) to God's people. The father of John had taught him that they were waiting and looking for the ***"Yeshua"*** of Israel who would save them from their sins. Then, John the Baptist confessed that the main reason behind his baptizing people in Jordan was to reveal Him (Yeshua/Jesus) to Israel as thus, *"And I knew him not; but that he should be manifest to Israel, therefore am I come baptizing with water"* (John 1:31).

John the Baptist was chosen to point the Jews or Israelites to a man called ***"Yeshua"*** or ***"Salvation"*** according to Luke 1:77. He took his time to point, direct and refer his people to the only man called **"YESHUA/JESUS"** as his ministerial assignment required. As John the Baptist grew up, his parents rehearsed in his ears the documented prophecy declared upon him by the Holy Spirit. The parents of John the Baptist taught their son and others in their synagogues and temple about ***'Yeshua/Yahshua' or the 'Salvation of Israel.'*** They also trained him by providing formal Jewish education. They made it known to John their son that God had chosen him to teach, preach and instruct the Jews about the man called ***Yeshua*** or ***Salvation of Israel***. The Holy Ghost gave him the ministry of water baptism so that through this means, he would manifest the ***Salvation/Yeshua of Israel*** to the children of Israel.

As ***Yeshua/Jesus*** came to be baptized in Jordan, John lifted up his voice and said to the Israelites, *"Behold the Lamb of God that takes away the sin of the world"* (John 1:29). The teaching ministry of John the Baptist hinged on manifesting the ***'Yeshua or Salvation'*** of Israel to the people of Israel. He declared to them that the Salvation/Yeshua/Jesus of Israel is the chosen Lamb of God who takes away the sin of the world (that land) in one day. This is revealed in the book of Zechariah 3:9, *"For behold the stone that I have laid before Joshua; upon one stone shall be seven eyes: behold, I will engrave the graving thereof, saith the LORD of hosts, and I will remove the iniquity of that land in one day."* You can now understand from the Bible that the ***"Salvation/Yeshua of Israel"*** is a **"Person"** and not a thing, a phenomenon or an event.

THE MAN SIMEON THE HIGH PRIEST AND CHRIST'S DEDICATION

The Holy Spirit led Simeon, the aged high priest, into the temple as Joseph and

Mary brought Him to Jerusalem for dedication. As he took the baby ***'Yeshua/Jesus'*** in his arms, he said, *"Lord, now lettest thou thy servant depart*

"SALVATION" which thou hast prepared before the face of all people; A light to lighten the Gentiles, and the glory of thy people Israel" (Luke2:29-32, emphasis mine).

for the consolation of Israel, did not speak in English, Greek or Latin language as he held God's Son in his arms for dedication but in Hebrew language. He said to the Father of the very Child he was carrying, *"My eyes have seen thine Salvation."*

Below is the accurate setting of this awesome revelation made by the high priest, *"Now Lord, you can let your servant depart, for my eyes have seen your* ***'Yeshua/Jesus.'***

This particular priest by name Simeon, who served the nation of Israel for many years in the things of God, studied under other priests who were before him about the expected ***Yeshua/Salvation*** of Israel. He also became a teacher, a priest and a professor of the ***Yeshua/Jesus/Salvation*** of Israel. The Bible tells us that he waited for the consolation of Israel. This "Consolation" of Israel is the very ***Yeshua/Salvation/Jesus*** whom he saw, touched and carried in his arms. As a priest in Israel, Simeon the high priest was a teacher and a custodian of the truth contained in God's word from Genesis to Malachi. *"For the priest's lips should keep knowledge and they should seek the law at his mouth: for he is the messenger of the LORD of hosts"* (Malachi 2:7). The ancient Hebrews sought the knowledge of the Person of Yeshua of Israel far above gold and all treasures in the world. They eagerly waited for the consolation of Israel, the Israelites and the whole world.

Every priest and generation of the Israelites all waited to see the ***Salvation*** or ***Yeshua*** of Israel made manifest in human body. The man who dedicated the ***Yeshua/Salvation*** of Israel to God Most High said that: (a) ***Yeshua/Salvation*** is a light that lights or illuminates the Gentiles (b) ***Yeshua*** is the glory of thy people Israel.

When we study God's ***Salvation/Yeshua*** according to the Scriptures, we are tactically studying the ***"Light"*** of the Gentiles and the ***"Glory"*** of the children of Israel. As Simeon the high priest prayed by the Holy Spirit while carrying the Man-Child in his hands he was saying to all the Israelites that this child in my hands is your ***Yeshua/Jesus.*** *This* is the implication of his prayers, 'Oh Israel, behold your **Yeshua/Jesus.'**

The true Salvation/Yeshua/Jesus of Israel is the Man—Child that Simeon dedicated in Jerusalem. In another development, Brother Glass Arthur shares his experience with us on the issue that is the most debated. He said that something very interesting occurred in one Spring in St. Louise: he said, *'I was sitting in the home of our friends, Brother and Mrs. Charles Siegelman, and another Jew was present there. He claimed Jewish Orthodoxy for his creed. Of course the discussion centers on* ***"Him"*** *who is the Creator of all things* ***Yeshua/Jesus of Israel."***

*This good Jewish brother opposed the claims of Yeshua in the Old Testament verbally and in a friendly fashion, most violently. His best offensive weapon, he thought was to fling at me and at all of us there, the well-known challenge, **"You cannot find the name of JESUS in the Old Testament" and this he did.***

*I did not answer him directly but asked him to translate for us from my Hebrew Bible **Isaiah 62:11**. Being a Hebrew scholar, he did so with utmost ease rapidly and correctly; and here is what and how he translated that text verbatim: "Behold thy Jehovah has proclaim unto the end of the world, Say ye to the daughter of Zion, Behold thy "YESHUA" (JESUS) cometh, behold His reward is with him, and His work before him."*

*Just then, he crimsoned as he realized what he had done and how he had played into my hands, and he just fairly screamed out "No! No! You made me read it "**THY YESHUA [JESUS]**." Mr. Glass! You tricked me! I said, no, I did not trick you. I just had you read the word of God for yourself. Can't you see that here **"SALVATION"** is a Person and not a thing or event? "He comes; "His reward is with "HIM" and "His work before Him." Then he rushed to his own Old Testament talking away frantically saying, "I am sure mine is different from yours. And when he found the passage, he just dropped like a deflated balloon. His Old Testament was of course identical. All he could use as an excuse was to deny the divine inspiration of the book of Isaiah.*

MR. GLASS' EXPERIENCE SIMILAR TO MINE

In many countries of the world today, many Orthodox Jews have received their academic courses in Judaism and they all ask the same question: ***"Where can we find JESUS in the Old Testament?"*** In the month of April 2014 at Nnewi in Anambra state of Nigeria, as I was discussing Jesus with a lady that is a member of Jehovah's Witness, she said to me that there is no place from Genesis to Malachi where the name **'Jesus'** appeared in the Old Testament Bible. After the discussion, I realized that this deeply seated ignorance in people's mind is a pandemonium that needs an urgent, a scholastic and detailed Biblical attention.

SETTING THE RECORDS STRAIGHT

"It is the glory of God to conceal a thing. But the honor of kings is to search out a matter" (Proverbs 25:2). The Almighty God has concealed the name of His Son **'JESUS'** the **'Christ'** in all the books in the Old Testament from Genesis to Malachi. This is His glory. In His infinite wisdom, He has committed His written word to His kings and priests so that they can search out the very matter He has concealed.

This is why His own Son has made us kings and priests unto His God and Father as the Scripture puts it, *"And hast made us kings and priests unto God and His Father: to him be glory and dominion forever and ever. Amen"* (Revelation 1:6)... *"And hast made us unto our God kings and priests: and we shall reign on the earth"* (Revelation 5:10).

We must give multiple attentions to God's Word especially whenever it repeats twice in a chapter. The import of His spoken and written Word whenever it echoes once or twice is the release of a divine power and energy that establishes His divine intent over people or things. *"God hath spoken once, twice have I heard this; that power belongeth unto God.* (Psalm62: 11). When God speaks once, it echoes twice, as King David stated in the above scripture.

This means that when God spoke once according to Revelation 1:6 on the issue of priesthood and kingship for us that it echoed twice. Then when He spoke again on the same issue of priesthood and kingship according to Revelation 5:10, it echoed four times. This is a divine principle: whenever God speaks once, it echoes twice. As He speaks twice, it echoes four times.

For two consecutive times God repeated Himself on the issue of the Church (Messianic Community) being made kings and priests by His Son Jesus Christ unto Himself. He made us kings and priests in order for us to fulfill the **(b) part of proverb 25: 2.** In God's eyes, it is a very great honour when His kings and priests search out matters He has hidden in His ancient Word so that the people would be delivered from confusion and deception. Just as the world rewards researchers and promotes them, likewise God also rewards His kings and priests who search and research the Bible through and through for them to have the light of the Holy Spirit and also import Christ's transcendental wisdom, knowledge, power, and riches to the people of the world.

Our own contribution to *"tikum ha olam"* (repairing of the world) is to depend on the Holy Spirit for Him to lead us into all the truth concerning our Master Jesus Christ as recorded in the Bible. We wish to set the records of the Bible about Him straight. *"The voice of him that crieth in the wilderness, prepare ye the way of the LORD, make straight in the desert a high way for our God"* (Isaiah 40:3).

There is a clarion call upon us to prepare the way of the **Lord Yeshua/ Jesus/Salvation** in these last days. This way goes beyond international standard of things. The Way of the Lord must be constructed according to heavenly standards using the tools of truth revealed and established in the Scriptures. *"Heaven demands a straight high way in the desert for our God."* Because of anti- Christ teachings by some orthodox Jews, so many souls of men have become a desert. God who took the Israelites through the desert as they left Egypt wants to have a high way in the desert of men's heart once again.

As He walks through those deserts of men's heart through the revealed truth about Yeshua/Jesus, all the cedars of lies and deceptions will be destroyed. In addition to this, the thick forests of wrong and false teachings that have grown for many years will also be consumed by the proactive knowledge of the Person of **Yeshua/Jesus** who is the only hope of Israel and the entire world.

"Every valley shall be exalted, and every mountain and hill shall be made low: and the crooked shall be made straight, and the rough places plain. And the glory of the LORD shall be revealed and all flesh sees it together: for the mouth of the LORD hath spoken it" (Isaiah 40:5).

Wrong education (i.e. education not based on the passages of the Bible) creates valleys in men's lives and at the same time, makes the recipients of such wrong education feel that they are at the top of the mountains and hills. The false teachings propagated by orthodox Jews against Jesus Christ of Nazareth have made so many of them to be crooked in heart and very rough in their attitude towards the very God of Abraham, Isaac and Israel and His Christ and genuine Christians. However, notwithstanding the damages that other Jews who do not believe in the Person of the Lord Jesus Christ of Nazareth have caused God, He still insists that every valley must be exalted.

We must fill up those valleys in men's heart with pure truth and knowledge of Christ Jesus. The mountains and hills are the false knowledge which have exalted themselves against the knowledge of God via Orthodox Judaism and secularism. Heaven demands that by means of searching out the concealed things of God, all the mountains and hills must be made low. Our Saviour Jesus Christ came to save the crooked and the rough people, but only the revealed truth of God's word preached and taught with deep love through priests and kings appointed by the Lamb can make crooked sinners straight and rough people plain.

There will be an awesome revelation of the glory of the Lord (Yahweh/Jehovah) as we who are the chosen generation of elect kings and priests begin to search out the deep mysteries of **Jesus/Yeshua** encoded in the Old Testament. The Holy Spirit wants us to pass this same knowledge through pro-active–teachings about Christ to our children at nursery who will in turn transfer such wealth of knowledge about *'Yeshua/ Jesus the Messiah'* to their own children. As we maintain the divine trend of transfer of deeply embedded wealth of knowledge of the **'Salvation/Yeshua/Jesus'** of Israel and the whole world, the glory of Yahweh/Jehovah/God will fill the earth as the waters cover the sea.

CHAPTER 4

BEST PRAYER FOR ORTHODOX JEWS

"To open their eyes, and to turn them from darkness to light, and from the power of Satan unto God, that they may receive forgiveness of sins, and inheritance among them which are sanctified by faith that is in me"
(Acts26: 18)

The best prayer that Messianic Jews and all Bible observant Christians must pray for the Orthodox Jews is that the God of all possibilities will begin to open their eyes to the true knowledge of the Salvation/Yeshua/Jesus of Israel because through Judaism, they have become partially blind. This partial blindness has kept them from finding **'YESHUA'** of Israel/Nazareth in their own Hebrew Bible from Genesis to Malachi. Many of the Orthodox Jews are under Satan's influence because of their unbelief in the Person of Yeshua/Jesus. Many of them are the adepts and princes of Freemason.

The most primary assignment our Yeshua/Jesus of Nazareth gave to Paul on his way to Damascus was to go and open the eyes of the Jews and Gentiles turn them from darkness to light and from the power of Satan to God. He has promised to forgive all the Jews who turn from Orthodox Judaism to Lord Yeshua/Jesus of Nazareth who is their only Christ.

He has an inheritance for all Jews who would embrace Yeshua/Jesus of Nazareth. As Apostle Paul embarked on the high calling of God upon his life, it was revealed to him that blindness in part had fallen on the unbelieving Jews. *"What then? Israel hath not obtained that which he seeketh for; but the election hath obtained it and the rest were blinded. According as written, God has given them the spirit of slumber, eyes that they should not see, and ears that they should not hear unto this day"* (Romans 11: 7-8).

The present spiritual condition of the Orthodox Jews is very pathetic and that is why they need our prayers for God to visit them and destroy the spirit of slumber, blindness and deafness among them. It is the spirit of blindness, deafness and slumber in every Orthodox Jewish person that keeps them from seeing their own Yeshua in their Tanakh or the Old Testament Scriptures. This spirit of slumber makes them to sleep on God's Word. The Jews are the chosen custodians of His Word in the Tanakh. However, the same spirit of deafness keeps them from hearing the truth of **Yeshua/Jesus** who has been coded in the very books of the Tanakh or the Old Testament Bible.

Many of the adepts and princes of Freemasonry are Orthodox Jews who have attained their 33rd degree in Freemasonic craft in search of the 'the Light' of Israel. They have not found 'that Light' even at 33rd degree because only **Yeshua/Jesus** of Nazareth who is Christ is the true **'Light of Israel and of the world'** as well the **'Glory of Israel'.**

Our Lord Jesus is the true Light of Israel as the Bible records it, *"And the light of Israel shall be for a fire, and his Holy One for a flame: and it shall burn and devour his thorns and briers in one day"* (Isaiah 10:17). He is the very Light that our brother, Apostle John spoke about in John 1:5-9, *"And the light (**the Light of Israel**) shineth in darkness; and the darkness comprehended it not. There was a man sent from God, whose name was John. The same came for a witness, to bear witness of the Light (the Light of Israel... Isaiah 10:17) that all men through him might believe. He was not that Light, but was sent to bear witness of that Light. That was the true Light, which lighteth every man that cometh into the world"* (Emphasis mine).

The other Jews of which greater numbers of them are Freemasons have cast aside Yeshua/Jesus the marvelous and bright Light of Israel. They have denied Him whom their fathers craved and waited for His coming as thus, *"For if their casting Yeshua aside means reconciliation for the world, what will their accepting him mean? It will be life from the dead"* (Romans 11:7 Complete Jewish Bible). The problem of Orthodox Jews is that they have cast aside ***Yeshua/Jesus*** of Israel who is also the true Light of Israel, the true Revealed Mystery of Israel and the Glory of Israel for many years. Their belief in their 'kabala' is their confusion and darkness. Since

John, the Baptist was not **'that Light of Israel,'** then, no man of the Jewish blood can claim to be ***'that Light.'***

Only our Master Yeshua/Jesus who is Christ is that ***'Light of Israel'*** who was revealed to Isaiah the prophet in chapter 10:17, of whom the apostles and prophets testify. The Illuminati may claim to be the *'enlightened ones'* yet they roam about in gross darkness because they have rejected *'Yeshua/Jesus of Nazareth the only true Light of Israel and their fathers.'* When the Illuminati (the falsely illuminated ones) and Freemasons (men and women bound by the deceptions of Lucifer) do not serve and worship Yeshua/Jesus Christ the true Light, that lights (illuminates) every man that comes into the world according to John 1:9, then the Illuminati and Freemasons are simply called ***"the grossly en-darkened ones."***

THE FIRST MESSAGE OF JESUS TO PAUL

A proper understanding of the first message our Lord Yeshua/Jesus the Christ to Paul and the language through which He communicated with him will help us resolve the problem of Orthodox Jews. *"And when we were all fallen to the earth, I heard a voice speaking to me, and saying in the Hebrew tongue, Saul, Saul, why persecutest thou me? It is hard for thee to kick against the prick. And I said, who art thou, Lord? And he said I am Jesus whom thou persecutest"* (Act26:14-15).

Originally, what we read in the Scripture above was a revelatory discussion in Hebrew language and not in English language. Therefore, if we approach this experience of Paul from the Hebrew language perspective, we would appreciate each point of the statement of Christ to Paul. Paul's name in Hebrew dialect is written and pronounced "Shaul" while Jesus' name is written and pronounced **'Yeshua/Yahshua.'** Therefore, in Hebrew dialect Paul heard a voice saying to him, "Shaul, Shaul why persecutest thou me?" Then in response to that question Shaul responded, "Who are thou Lord?" Then in answer to Shaul's question the Master said to him, **"I am Yeshua/Yahshua/Jesus"** whom thou persecutest.

When our brother Paul heard this name "Yeshua" from the Light above the brightness of the sun, he knew whom He was that talked with him. Paul was a student of the law in the Tanakh/Old Testament under a prominent doctor in the law of God by name Gamaliel. In the educational pursuit of the Jews as providence required, every Jewish person studied in depth their Jewish laws. They all studied the prophecies of their father Israel as well as the prophecies of their prophets such as Moses, Samuel, David, Isaiah, Jeremiah, Habakkuk and the entire priests who prophesied about the coming of the ***"Salvation"*** of Israel as revealed in Genesis 49:18 which states, *"I have waited for thy salvation O LORD."*

When their patriarchal father by name Israel blessed his twelve sons, he blessed them in Hebrew language. So, Genesis 49:18 would read in Hebrew native language, *"I have waited for thy 'Yeshua' O LORD."*

The "Salvation" that Israel who was the grandson of Abraham was waiting for is a Person and not an event. All the Israelites were told to wait for God's ***"Yeshua/Salvation/Jesus*** of Nazareth, as we will see very shortly. The knowledge of Salvation/Yeshua/Jesus of Israel was and is still the central curriculum of all the Israelites beginning with the twelve sons of Israel to their offspring.

Therefore, the first message that Apostle Paul receive on his way to Damascus was the message and revelation of "Yeshua/Jesus" of Israel. As Paul was restored after experiencing the awesome and amazing light from ***"Salvation/Yeshua of Israel"*** that struck him blind for three days, he went about preaching to them that **"Yeshua/Jesus"** of Nazareth/Israel has appeared to him in the Person of a 'Bright Light', which is far above the brightness of the sun. He began to prove to them that Yeshua/Jesus of Nazareth was the very Christ.

MOSES AND YESHUA /JESUS OF ISRAEL

"And Moses said unto the people, fear ye not, stand still, and see ye the <u>salvation</u> of the LORD, which he will show to you today: for the Egyptians which ye have seen today, ye shall see them again no more forever" (Genesis 14:13, Emphasis mine).

When the Israelites left Egypt on the 15th day of Abib in the 430th year of their captivity, the Egyptians pursued after them to destroy them. It was at this point that Jehovah ordered the Israelites through Moses to fear not but rather stand still and see the **'Salvation or Yeshua'** of the LORD. Immediately, Yeshua/Jesus of the LORD who is also called the Salvation/Yeshua of Israel appeared to save them. Here, Moses and the Israelites saw the Salvation/Yeshua /Jesus of the LORD as He delivered them from the Egyptians.

MOSES AND HIS SYMPHONIC SONG OF DELIVERANCE

"The LORD is my strength and my song, and he is become my salvation. He is my God and I will prepare him a habitation; my father's God and I will exalt him" (Exodus 15:2, Emphasis mine).

In this Scripture, Moses revealed the most awesome mysteries of our Lord Jesus Christ. He said that Jehovah (THE LORD) is his strength and song. He also said that Yahweh/Jehovah has become his **'Salvation.'** We must agree with the fact that Moses sang this song in Hebrew dialect and not in English or Greek language. Therefore, the proper rendering of the second part of this verse of the Scripture would be, **'Yahweh/Jehovah/The LORD has become my Yeshua/Jesus.'** Our brother Moses knew that Yahweh/Jehovah is the Yeshua/Jesus of Israel their ancestor and his offspring. He said that Yeshua/Jesus is his God and that he (Moses) would build Him a habitation. He also said that Yahweh/Jehovah who has become his Yeshua is his father's God. This implies that Amram who was the biological father of Moses knew and served Yeshua/Jesus of Israel. Furthermore, He promised to exalt him. Moses' father by name Amram knew Yeshua of Israel and waited for him to come according to God's promise to Israel their father.

REVEALED MYSTERIES IN THE OLD AND NEW TESTAMENTS

OLD TESTAMENT		NEW TESTAMENT
"YAHWEH/JEHOVA HAS BECOME MY SALVATION/YESHUA/JESUS " (EXODUS 15:2)		"AND THE WORD BECAME FLESH AND DWELT AMONG US" (JOHN1:14)

The Spirit of the Almighty God revealed to Moses that Yahweh/Jehovah would one day become their Yeshua/Jesus in human form; the very revelation of Yahweh/Jehovah becoming our "Salvation" who is Yeshua/Jesus was also given to King David according to Psalm 118:14. Our brother John the Beloved bears witness about the fulfillment of Exodus 15:2. He said that the **"WORD"** became a human being and dwelt among us.

By implication and thorough analysis, Yahweh/Jehovah who became Moses' **Yeshua/Jesus** is also the same **'WORD'** in John1:1 and 14, who has become flesh and dwells among us.

Therefore, the Salvation/Yeshua/Jesus of Israel who is Yahweh/Jehovah is the same person called the "WORD." Our brother Moses who wrote the books of Genesis, Exodus, Leviticus, Numbers and Deuteronomy, wrote them in Hebrew language. Prior to the coming of Christ and afterwards, the highest point of studies in the land of Israel concentrated on the 'Consolation of Israel.' The knowledge of the coming of **'Yeshua/Jesus'** of Israel who would save them and the entire world from Satan and all troubles, was their national curriculum of studies at kinder, primary, secondary and tertiary institutions of learning.

CHAPTER 5

YESHUA/JESUS REVEALED IN THE BOOK OF PSALMS

The Spirit of the Almighty God gave each book of the Bible to His people by the inspiration of the Almighty and its essence is to reveal the person of the **"Salvation/Yeshua of Israel"** to all the descendants of Israel. The descendants of Israel are the chosen of God with the primary assignment to spread the knowledge of "YESHUA" of Israel to the rest of the nations of the world. Every man and woman in Israel is required to study this national course on **'Salvation/Yeshua of Israel.'** Biblically and historically, every victory the Israelites recorded has their source from help received from the **'Salvation/Yeshua of Israel'** whom we call Jesus of Nazareth today.

The most famous King of Israel by name King David had his childhood education on the coming of Yeshua/Jesus of Israel, under such tutors and governors as Samuel, Jesse and others. He was acquainted and properly furnished with the knowledge that the Saviour of Israel would come in human flesh and so he championed the course of Yeshua/Jesus of Israel in his days. The heart cry of King David was that the ***"Salvation /Yeshua of Israel"*** would come as revealed in the Scriptures below.

"Oh that the salvation of Israel were come out of Zion! When the LORD bringeth back the captivity of his people, Jacob shall rejoice, and Israel shall be glad" (Psalm14:7). If you read this chapter and verse of the Bible in its original Hebrew text and then translate it from Hebrew language to English language, it would read, ***"Oh that the 'Yeshua/Jesus' of Israel were come out of Zion!"*** May I add here that although it is obvious that majority of the Israelites do not know nor acknowledge their *Salvation/Yeshua/Jesus*, yet He has been faithful to them.

KING DAVID AND HIS PRIMARY CALLING

"O God thou hast taught me from my youth: and hitherto have I declared your wondrous work" (Psalm 71:17). All the great leaders in Israel were people who were taught by God from their youths. In their academic pursuit, the primary focus was on the **'Salvation/Yeshua of Israel.'** Their testimony focused on how Yeshua/Jesus saved their father Israel from the hands of his brother Esau and other enemies. They were students of Yeshua/Jesus of Israel and conservators of the great truth of all ages— *the coming of the salvation of Israel into the world.* The utmost goal of every Jewish father was to transmit the knowledge of the **"Salvation/Yeshua/Jesus"** of Israel to their children who would in turn transfer it to their own children until the physical revelation of Yeshua/Jesus of Israel whose birth took place in Bethlehem Ephratah.

"That the generation to come might know them, even the children which should be born" (Psalm 78:6). As far as our brief life allows us to arrange, we must industriously provide for the godly nature of youth. God's commands and doctrines are calculated to exert an influence as long as our race exists.

The second part of the scripture above says, *"Which should arise and declare them to their children..."* The one object aimed at is transmission. The testimony and revelation of the **Salvation/Yeshua/Jesus** of Israel is only given that it may be passed on to the succeeding generations.

This is what the Psalmist revealed in Psalm 78:70-72, *"He chose David also his servant, and took him from the sheepfolds; from following the ewes great with young, he brought him to feed Jacob his people, and Israel his inheritance. So he fed them according to the integrity of his heart; and guided them by the skillfulness of his hands."*

The primary election upon David was for him to be a warrior-king and a teaching-king in Israel for the purpose of transmission of the knowledge of the Salvation/Yeshua/Jesus of Israel and His imminent coming out of Zion to the earth. It was an election of sovereign gracious kind, and it operated practically by making the chosen man a willing servant of the LORD. It is wonderful how often-divine wisdom so arranges the early and obscure portion of a choice life, to make it a preparatory school for more active and noble future.

The noblest election of God invested upon King David was for him to feed the Israelites with the knowledge and certainty of the **Salvation/Yeshua** of Israel. God committed His Word to King David for conservation. He was born to live by the Word of God and any slightest deviation from God's Word brought heavy affliction on him because the primary reason he was born and chosen was for him to be a teacher of the people in the core knowledge of the Salvation/Yeshua/Jesus of Israel. *"Before I was afflicted, I went astray; but now have I kept your word"* (Psalm 119:67).

When we hear that king David was a man after God's heart, it means that he was a man who sought after the **'Salvation of Israel'** and the truth that proceeded out of God's heart. The Salvation of Israel is the *"Central-Heart of the Father for all men and whosoever seeks Him i.e. Jesus, touches the heart of the Father in heaven."* To be after God's heart is to be after His Salvation/Yeshua/Jesus who is also His Word that has become flesh. King David revealed and taught his own fellow nationals and the people from other nations who used to come for God's feasts in Jerusalem, **'the Yeshua of Israel'** and how awesome He is.

In Psalm 53:6, the king repeated exactly the same prayer he prayed in Psalm 14:7 as thus *"Oh that the salvation of Israel would come out of Zion! When God bringeth again the captivity of his people, Jacob shall rejoice, and Israel shall be glad."* If you translate Psalm 53:6 from a Hebrew Bible, the word salvation reads "Yeshua." Therefore, he prayed again as thus, *"Oh that* ***the Yeshua*** *of Israel would come out of Zion."* In all the generations of the fathers of Israel, they all waited to see that blessed One— Yeshua/Jesus of Israel as they were promised by the immutable God. The utmost hope and the consolation of every Israelite is the coming of the **Salvation/Yeshua /Jesus of Israel** out of Zion.

THE PRAYER OF KING DAVID

"Restore unto me the joy of thy salvation, and uphold me with thy free spirit" (Psalm51:12, Emphasis mine). If you read the Scripture above, you will realize that King David requested before God the Father to restore unto him the joy of "His Salvation" which is called in Hebrew language "Yeshua." He did not request God to restore unto him his life, lost gold or lost friends but rather the joy of ***"His Yeshua."*** Please, take note of the phrase, **"Thy Salvation"** which is the same as **"Thy Yeshua" or "Thy Jesus."** Yeshua or Jesus of Nazareth is the only joy of the world.

David lost both God's Salvation/Yeshua and His joy at his offence against Uriah and Bathsheba because of fornication and murder. Those who belong to the Salvation/Yeshua/Jesus of Israel must live at His standards of life, righteousness, and justice. It is not enough to have a common knowledge of the **'Salvation/Yeshua of Israel'** and not to live by His terms. Saul (now Paul) who possibly had some degrees in the studies of Jewish laws and prophets, attained to the level where he was commissioned a zealot to the faith of their fathers. His zeal for the preservation of the traditional faith of their fathers turned him into a murderer. He had killed the saints of Christ in ignorance in trying to defend their traditional belief. This observation above is also the same with so many other Jews who in their zeal to defend the traditional Judaism of their fathers have committed heinous crimes against the **Salvation/Yeshua/Jesus** of Israel/Nazareth.

The same **Salvation** of Israel is also called **Peace.** Peace (Shalom) is a Person and not just a feeling or a state of absence of chaos. When the people of the book greet one another with the word **'Shalom',** they are wishing each other the **"Salvation/Yeshua"** who alone is their high hope. However, the question we must ask ourselves is this, 'do majority of the Jews really have **Yeshua/Jesus** of Nazareth in their lives, families, and communities?' The **Salvation/Yeshua of Israel** dwells only where He is recognized and worshipped.

Naturally, whenever a man embraces **Jesus/Yeshua/Jesus of Israel**, great joy fills his heart. The greatest loss any man or woman can record is the loss of the **"Salvation/Yeshua"** of God and Israel out of his heart. One cannot understand the pain of this loss of Salvation/Yeshua's joy if he has never experienced Him before. King David had Him before but when he lost Him, he cried to have Him back.

If King David who was placed very high in Israel, would cry for God to restore unto him the joy of God's **Salvation/Yeshua/Jesus,** then all the Orthodox Jews must turn from their foolishness amid their accumulated wealth and ask the living God for the joy of ***"His Yeshua/Jesus of Nazareth to be restored to them.***

DETAILED REVELATION OF YESHUA/JESUS IN THE BOOK OF PSALMS

"We will rejoice in thy salvation, and in the name of our God, we will set up our banners: the LORD fulfills all thy petitions" (Psalm 20:5). If you read the book of apostles, you will realize that most of the references there were culled from the

book of Psalms. All the disciples were students of the book of Psalms and other books of the Old Testament. They all knew the name **"Yeshua"** which English translates as **"JESUS".** This name **"Yeshua"** is a household name that the Jews held in high esteem as they studied the written prophecies of the fathers and prophets. In the Scripture above, one of their fathers by name, King David who was a prophet and a sweet Psalmist admonished all the Israelites and their future children to rejoice in **God's Yeshua**, who is called **Salvation** by translation. They rejoiced in the **Yeshua of Israel** because he saved their fathers and all their children as well.

"The LORD is my light and my salvation: whom shall I fear? The LORD is the strength of my life, of whom shall I be afraid?" (Psalm 27:10).

Here, King David revealed to the Israelites whom he fed with the pure knowledge of God's nature and word that Jehovah is his light and salvation.

This implies that Jehovah/Yahweh is his light and **"Yeshua/Jesus."** Moses also said that Jehovah/Yahweh has become his **Salvation/Yeshua/Jesus**. Therefore, from the above Scripture, since the LORD/Jehovah/Yahweh is the Light and Yeshua, it means that Jehovah/Yahweh is the same Person called Yeshua/Jesus in the New Testament. This revelation is certain and the allegory very sure.

It was at the mouth of Moses according to Exodus 15:2 and King David according to Psalm 27:1 that this irrevocable matter is established .i.e. Jehovah/Yahweh is Yeshua/Jesus/Salvation of Nazareth. This coherence in the teachings of the two greatest leaders in Israel namely Moses and King David dissolves the most heated debate about the pre-existence of Jesus in the Old Testament.

Chapter 6

WAITERS ON YAHWEH/JEHOVAH/THE LORD

As you read through the book of Psalms, you will appreciate the words of admonition of King David by God's Spirit to the Israelites who waited to see also the LORD's Salvation of Israel as thus: *"Wait on the LORD: be of good courage, and he shall strengthen thine heart: wait, I say, on the LORD"*. (Psalm 27:14).
This great King by name David, expounded Genesis 49:18 to the people. He was used greatly to strengthen the hearts of the children of Israel just as Israel their father also did. He commanded them to wait on the coming of the Yeshua/Jesus of Israel.

THE REVELATION OF JESUS IN THE BOOK OF PSALMS

"Draw out also the spear; and stop the way against them that persecute me; and say unto my soul, I am thy salvation" (Psalm 35:3). *Interpretation: The Psalmist here cried to Jehovah telling Him to take His spear and stop his pursuers. He also requested from Yahweh/Jehovah to say to him, "I am thy Salvation/Yeshua/Jesus.

"And my soul shall be joyful in the LORD; it shall rejoice in His salvation" (Psalm 35:9, Emphasis mine)
*Interpretation: My soul shall be joyful in Jehovah/Yahweh; it shall rejoice in His Yeshua/Jesus.

"I have not hid thy righteousness within my heart; I have declared thy faithfulness and thy salvation; I have not concealed thy loving kindness and thy truth from the great congregation" (Psalm 40:10, Emphasis mine)... *Interpretation: I have not hid your righteousness (Tzaddik) within my heart; I have declared thy faithfulness and thy Yeshua; I have not concealed thy loving kindness and thy truth from the great congregation.

"Let all those that seek thee rejoice and be glad in thee. Let such as love thy salvation say continually, the LORD be magnified" (Psalm 40:16, Emphasis mine).

*Interpretation: Let all those that seek thee rejoice and be glad in thee; let such as love thy **"Yeshua/Jesus"** say continually, Jehovah/Yahweh be magnified.

"Whoso offereth praise glorifieth me: and to him that ordereth his conversation aright will I shew the salvation of God" (Psalm 50:23, Emphasis mine).
*Interpretation: Whoso offers praise glorifies me: and to him that orders his conversation aright will I show the **Yeshua/Jesus** of God.

The reason our heavenly Father showed His **Yeshua/Jesus** to Simeon and chose him to dedicate His beloved Son to Him was that Simeon had the profile of righteousness required of God according to Psalm 50:23. *"And behold there was a man in Jerusalem, whose name was Simeon and the same was just and devote waiting for the consolation of Israel; and the Holy Ghost was upon Him"* (Luke 2:25).

"Truly my soul waited upon God, from him cometh my salvation" (Psalm 62:1, Emphasis mine).
*Interpretation: Truly my soul waits upon God from Him comes my **Yeshua/Jesus**.

"He only is my rock and salvation; he is my defense; I shall not be greatly moved" (Psalm 62:26, Emphasis mine).
*Interpretation: He is my rock and **"Yeshua/Jesus"** and He is my defense, I shall not be greatly moved.

"In God is my salvation and my glory; the rock of my strength, and my refuge, is in God" (Psalm 62:7, Emphasis mine).
*Interpretation: In God is my **"Yeshua/Jesus"** and my glory, the rock of my strength and my refuge is in God. The just and devout man by name Simeon said that **Yeshua/Jesus** is a Light that lightens the Gentiles and the glory of thy people Israel.

"By terrible things in righteousness wilt thou answer us, O God of our salvation; who art the confidence of the ends of the earth, and of them that are afar off upon the sea" (Psalm 65:5, Emphasis mine). *Interpretation: By terrible things in righteousness will you answer us, O God of our **"Yeshua/Jesus;** who is the confidence of all the ends of the earth, and of them that are afar off upon the sea.

"Blessed be the Lord, who daily loadeth us with benefits, even the God of our salvation" (Psalm 68:19, KJV).

*Interpretation: Blessed be the Lord, who daily loads us with benefits, even the God of our **Yeshua/Jesus.**

"He that is our God is the God of salvation; and unto God the LORD belongeth issues from death" (Psalm 68:20).
*Interpretation: He that is our God is the God of **Yeshua/Jesus;** and unto God, the Lord belongs issues from death.

"But as for me, my prayer is unto thee; O Lord in an acceptable time, O God in the multitude of thy mercy hear me, in the truth of thy salvation"
(Psalm 69:13, KJV).
*Interpretation: But as for me, my prayer is unto you, O Lord, in an acceptable time; O God in the multitude of thy mercy, hear me in the truth of thy **"Yeshua/Jesus."** Please note very well that God Almighty can only hear us if we uphold the truth of His Son Yeshua of Nazareth.

"My mouth shall show forth thy righteousness and thy salvation all the day; for I know not the numbers of them" (Psalm 71:15, KJV).
*Interpretation: My mouth shall show forth thy Tzaddik and thy **Yeshua** all the day; for I do not know the numbers of them. Take note of this: The word **'Righteousness'** is called in Hebrew language**, 'Tzaddik'** while the word **'Salvation'** is called in the same Hebrew language, **'Yeshua.'**

"Because they believed not in God, and trusted not in His Salvation"
(Psalm 78:22).
*Interpretation: Because they believe not in God and trusted not in His **Yeshua/Jesus.** Although Moses had told them that Jehovah/Yahweh has become their Yeshua/Jesus, yet they did not believe in God's **Yeshua**, but rejected Him until date. *"And he came unto his own, and his own received him not"* (John 1:11).

"Help us, O God of our salvation, for the glory of thy name; and deliver us, and purge away our sins, for thy name's sake" (Psalm 79:9).

*Interpretation: Help us, O God of our **Yeshua/Jesus,** for the glory of thy name and deliver us, and purge away our sins, for thy name's sake.

"Turn us O God of our salvation, and cause thine anger towards us to cease (Psalm 85:4).
*Interpretation: Turn us O God of our **Yeshua/Jesus** and cause thine anger towards us to cease.

"Shew us mercy and grant us thy salvation" **(Psalm 85:7).** *Interpretation: Show us mercy and grant us or allow your **Yeshua/Jesus** to come to us.
"Surely, his salvation is nigh them that fear him; that glory may dwell in our land" (Psalm 85:9).
*Interpretation: Assuredly, God's **Yeshua/Jesus** is near unto them that fear him that glory may dwell in our land.

"O LORD God of my salvation, I have cried day and night before thee
(Psalm 88:1).
*Interpretation: O LORD God of my **Yeshua/Jesus**, I have cried day and night before thee.

"He shall cry unto me, thou art my father, my God and the rock of my salvation" (Psalm 89:26).
*Interpretation: He shall cry to me, thou art my Father, my God and the rock of my **Yeshua /Jesus.**

"With long life will I satisfy him and shew him my salvation" (Psalm 91:16). *Interpretation: With long life will I satisfy him and show him my **Yeshua/Jesus.**

"O come, let us sing unto the LORD: let us make a joyful noise to the rock of our salvation" (Psalm 95:1).
*Interpretation: O come, let us sing unto the LORD, let us make a joyful noise to the rock of our **Yeshua/ Jesus.**

"Sing unto the LORD, bless his name, shew forth his salvation from day to day" (Psalm 96:2).
*Interpretation: Sing unto Jehovah, bless His name: show forth His **Yeshua/Jesus** from day to day. The primary purpose of all the saints of the Most High God from Adam to Simeon the priest was to show forth our heavenly Father's Yeshua/Jesus from day to day. This is also our calling. We must go and show forth our heavenly Father's Yeshua/Jesus of Israel/Nazareth to the world and Orthodox Jews.

"The LORD hath made known his salvation: his righteousness hath he openly shewed in the sight of the heathen" (Psalm 98:2).
*Interpretation: Jehovah has made known **His Yeshua/Jesus:** His righteousness (Tzaddik) hath he openly showed in the sight of the heathen. *"And Pilate wrote a title, and put it on the cross. And the writing was, JESUS OF NAZARETH THE KING OF THE JEWS: This title read many of the Jews for the place where Jesus was crucified*

was nigh to the city: and it was written in Hebrew and Greek, and Latin" (John 19:19-20).

By proper interpretation, this is what Pilate wrote over the cross of our Lord and Savior Jesus/Yeshua:

❖ *In Hebrew Pilate wrote, "This is* ***"Yeshua"*** *of Nazareth the King of the Jews.*

❖ In Greek, he wrote, "This is **"Iésous"** of Nazareth the King of the Jews.

❖ In Latin, he wrote, "This is **"Iesus"** of Nazareth the King of the Jews. If Pilate were in our time, he would have written it in English language as thus; ***"This is Jesus of Nazareth the King of the Jews."*** For example, in German, the English word for **'book'** is ***'buch.'*** In Spanish, it is called ***'libro'*** and in French, it is called **'livre.'** The language changes but the **'object'** itself does not change. Therefore, in the same way we can refer to Jesus as **"Iesus, Iésous or 'Yeshua/ Yahshua"** without changing His nature.

"He hath remembered his mercy and his truth towards the house of Israel: all the ends of the earth have seen the salvation of our God" (Psalm 98:3). *Interpretation: He has remembered His mercy and His truth towards the house of Israel: all the ends of the earth have seen the **"Yeshua /Jesus** of our God.

"... all the ends of the earth have seen the salvation of our God" (Psalm 98:3). Greek and Latin were the dominant languages during the days of Christ, and God as it were, used Pilate to send a telegraph to the ends of the world in their own languages saying..., behold the **Salvation/Yeshua** of Israel. All of you, who want to be members of the Commonwealth of Israel, behold Him.

This fact is not only recorded in the New Testament book of the Bible. It is in the history of Israel as well as the Roman empire chronicles, thereby fulfilling the scripture; *"The LORD hath made bare his holy arm in the eyes of all the nations; and all the ends of the earth shall see the salvation of our God"* (Isaiah 52:10). Making bare the holy arm here means to be generous. God generously introduced His Salvation/Yeshua/Jesus to the world on the Cross of Calvary that we might believe in Him and be saved.

"I will take the cup of salvation, and call upon the name of the LORD"
(Psalm 116:13).

*Interpretation: I will take the cup of **Yeshua/Jesus** and I will call upon the name of Jehovah/Yahweh. For a deeper insight into the cup of Salvation/Yeshua/Jesus, let us see the following chapters in the New

Testament. *"And he took the cup and gave thanks, and gave it to them saying, Drink ye all of it; For this is my blood of the new testament which is shed for many for the remission of sins"* (Mathew 26:27-28)... *"And he took the cup, and when he had given thanks, he gave it to them: and they all drank of it"* (Mark14:23)... *"Likewise also the cup after the supper saying, this cup is the new testament in my blood, which is shed for you"* (Luke 22:20).

The word ***'the cup'*** denotes a definite article. From Mathew 26:27-28 to Mark 14:23 and even to Luke 22:20, **'the cup'** is particular. The cup that our King Yeshua/Jesus gave to His disciple was the fulfillment of **Psalm 116:13.** Each of the disciples took that cup of **Salvation/Yeshua/Jesus** and drank from it. Today, our King **Yeshua/Salvation/Jesus** is also offering this cup to His chosen ones.

"The LORD is my strength and song, and is become my salvation" (Psalm 118:14).
*Interpretation: Jehovah is my strength and song, and is become my **Yeshua/Jesus.**

"The voice of rejoicing and salvation is in the tabernacle of the righteous: the right hand of the LORD doeth valiantly" (Psalm 118:15).
*Interpretation: The voice of rejoicing and **Yeshua/Jesus** is in the tabernacle of the righteous: the right hand of the LORD does wonderfully.

"I will praise thee: for thou hast heard me, and art become my salvation"
(Psalm 118:21).
*Interpretation: I will praise you: for you have heard me, and art become my **Yeshua/Jesus.**

"Let thy mercies come unto me, O LORD, even thy salvation according to thy word"
(Psalm 119:41).
*Interpretation: Let your mercies come unto me O Jehovah even your **"Yeshua/Jesus** according to your word.

"Mine eyes fail for thy salvation and for the word of thy righteousness"
(Psalm 119:123).
*Interpretation: My eyes fail for your **Yeshua/Jesus** and for the word of your righteousness (Tzaddik).

"Salvation is far from the wicked: for they seek not thy statutes" (Psalm 119:155).
*Interpretation: **"Yeshua/Jesus** is far from the wicked: for they seek not your statutes.

"LORD, I have hoped for thy salvation and done thy commandments"
(Psalm 119:166).
*Interpretation: Jehovah, I have Hoped for your **Yeshua/Jesus** and done thy commandments.

"I have longed for thy salvation, O LORD; and thy law is my delight"
(Psalm 119:166).

*Interpretation: I have longed for your **Yeshua/Jesus;** O Jehovah/Yahweh; and thy law is my delight.

"O God the Lord the strength of my salvation thou hast covered my head in the day of battle" (Psalm 140:7).

*Interpretation: O God the LORD, the strength of my **Yeshua/Jesus** you have covered my head in the day of battle.

"It is he that giveth salvation unto kings: who delivered David his servant from the hurtful sword" (Psalm 144:10).

*Interpretation: It is He that gives **Yeshua/Jesus** unto kings: who delivered David from the hurtful sword.

This verse is deep in mystery. Our heavenly Father by His Holy Spirit gives ***Yeshua/Jesus of Nazareth/Israel*** to all the kings of the earth. He is the utmost gift of the living God of Abraham, Isaac and Israel to kings and leaders of the earth. Every king or leader that desires to be successful must receive ***Yeshua/Jesus of Israel/Nazareth*** into his life, family, government and nation. Failed kings and leaders in Israel and the world today are those who refuse ***Yeshua/Jesus of Israel/Nazareth.***

"For the LORD taketh pleasure in his people: he will beautify the meek with salvation" (Psalm 144:4).
*Interpretation: For Jehovah takes pleasure in His people: He will beautify the meek with **Yeshua/Jesus.** Through Yeshua/Jesus, our Messiah the Holy Ghost beautifies the meek. The meek of the earth are only those men and women who have received Yeshua/Jesus of Israel/Nazareth. Through Him, the Holy Ghost changes their ugliness into beauty in the Father's eyes.

All the holy men that were called to write the Holy Scriptures especially the book of Psalms namely, King David, Asaph and Korah had **'Yeshua/Jesus of Israel'** as their number one primary and professional goal. That is why our King and Lord **Yeshua/Jesus** said we should search the Scriptures for they speak about Him.

CHAPTER 7

YESHUA/JESUS OF ISRAEL CODED IN THE BOOK OF ISAIAH WITH THE WORD 'SALVATION'

Prophet Isaiah's central revelation and writings focused primarily on the "Salvation" of our God to Israel. The Holy Ghost who was in each of those holy prophets spoke through them as He pointed all the Israelites and the Gentiles to the **"Salvation"** ready to be revealed. The prophet Isaiah spoke extensively and wrote intensively on the Person of **"Salvation of Israel"** as we will later see in details.

"Behold, God is my salvation, I will trust and not be afraid: for the LORD Jehovah is my strength and my song; he is also become my salvation" (Isaiah 12:2). Here, the prophet said, *"Behold God is my salvation."*

*Interpretation/Application: Behold God is my **Yeshua/Jesus.** He said that the Almighty God is His **Yeshua/Jesus.** He said that the LORD/Jehovah has also become his ***'Salvation/Yeshua /Jesus.'***

"Therefore with joy shall ye draw water out of the wells of salvation" (Isaiah 12:3).
*Interpretation/Application: The prophecy reveals that we can only approach **Yeshua/Jesus** with joy in order for us to draw water from the wells (the wounds, the bruises, chastisement and stripes) of ***Salvation/Yeshua/Jesus.*** Here the Holy Ghost revealed to Isaiah that Yeshua/Jesus of Israel/Nazareth would establish wells of water for us much higher and deeper than the wells of Jacob. The wells of **Yeshua/Jesus** are His wounds, bruises, chastisements and stripes, which were established through His awful sufferings as He paid the price of redemption for our sins. *"But one of the soldiers with a spear pierced his side, and forthwith came there out blood and water"* (John 19:34).

In the heart of **Yeshua/Jesus** of Israel/Nazareth who has also become our Passover and Atonement Lamb, are deep and mighty wells, from which living blood and waters flow. In a vision, prophet Isaiah foresaw the breaking of the body of **Salvation/Yeshua/Jesus** of Israel by the Roman soldiers as living wells out of which we must draw living water and blood with joy.

"And it shall be said in that day, Lo, this is our God; we have waited for him; and he will save us: this is the LORD: we have waited for him; we will be glad and rejoice in his salvation" (Isaiah 25:9).
*Interpretation: And it shall be said in that day, Lo, this is our God: we have waited for Him and He will save us: this is ***JEHOVAH/YAHWEH:*** we have waited for Him; we will be glad and rejoice in His **Yeshua/Jesus.**

We must bear in mind that the patriarch by name Israel who was the father of all the Israelites was the first to ignite this fiery hope of waiting for our everlasting Father of Israel called ***"Salvation/Yeshua."*** Today, many Jews have come to agree that the very ***'Salvation/Yeshua'*** that Israel their father waited for is the very Person spoken about in Isaiah 25:9. This **Salvation/Yeshua** is both our God and Jehovah/Yahweh.

"In that day shall this song be sung in the land of Judah; we have a strong city; salvation will God appoint for walls and bulwarks" (Isaiah 26:1).
*Interpretation: In that day shall this song be sung in the land of Judah; we have a strong city; **Yeshua/Jesus** will God appoint for the walls and bulwarks.

Application: For the strong city of Judah, God the Father appointed **"Yeshua/Jesus"** of Israel to be the defense of its walls and bulwarks. Only ***Yeshua/Jesus of Israel/Nazareth*** has been appointed by our heavenly Father to keep and defend Judah, Jerusalem, Israel and the whole world, hence the name ***"The Lion of the Tribe of Judah."*** In the book of Hebrews, God the Father has appointed Yeshua/Jesus who is His only begotten Son to be the inheritor of Judah, Jerusalem, Israel and complete wide world in fulfillment of Isaiah 26:1.

"But Israel shall be saved in the LORD with everlasting salvation. Ye shall not be ashamed nor confounded world without end" (Isaiah 45:17, emphasis mine).
*Interpretation: But Israel shall be saved in Jehovah with **"everlasting Yeshua/Jesus."** You, Israel shall not be ashamed or confounded forever and ever.

Our heavenly Father has assured the nation of Israel that He would save them from their troubles and enemies as they become united with "**everlasting Yeshua/ Jesus of Nazareth.**" God Almighty assures the Israelites and the entire world that, they will not be ashamed or confounded forever and ever, by accepting the "**everlasting Yeshua/Jesus**" and becoming united with Him. It is in union with "*everlasting Salvation/Yeshua/Jesus of Israel/Nazareth* that we all will be saved from Satan and his wicked spirits.

"I bring near my righteousness; it shall not be far off, and my salvation shall not tarry: and I will place salvation in Zion for Israel my glory" (Isaiah 46:13).
*Interpretation: I bring near my righteousness (Tzaddik); He shall not be far off and my **"Yeshua"** shall not tarry. I will place **Yeshua/Jesus** in Zion for Israel my glory. Our heavenly Father has expressly brought near His 'Righteousness' (Tzaddik) and 'Salvation' (Yeshua) in the person of His beloved Son and has placed the same **Yeshua/Jesus** in Zion, which is earthly Jerusalem. In Zion i.e. earthly Jerusalem, we saw God as He placed **'His Yeshua'** in the hands of Simeon the high priest who also waited for the consolation of Israel. Are you an Israelite or a Gentile, please can you just allow the Holy Ghost to place **'Yeshua/Jesus'** of Nazareth in your own hands and heart forever?

"And he said, it is a light thing that thou shouldest be my servant to raise up the tribes of Jacob; and also restore the preserved of Israel: I will also give thee to be a light to the Gentiles, and that thou mayest be my salvation unto the end of the earth" (Isaiah 49:6).

*Interpretation: And He said, it is a light thing that you should be my servant to raise up the tribes of Jacob, and to restore the preserved of Israel. I will also give thee to be light to the Gentiles (see Luke 2:32a) and that you may be my **"Yeshua/Jesus"** unto the end of the earth. This prophecy is the direct word of God the Father to His Son Jesus Christ. In this discourse, heaven invited prophet Isaiah to this all-important meeting of the Trinity to bear witness of the Father's Word to His beloved Son **Yeshua/Jesus.**

"Thus saith the LORD, in an acceptable time have I heard thee, and in the day of salvation have I helped thee: and I will preserve thee and give thee for a covenant of the people to establish the earth, to cause to inherit the desolated heritages" (Isaiah 49:8).

*Interpretation: Thus says Jehovah the Father, in an acceptable time have I heard you. In the day of ***"Yeshua/Jesus",*** I have helped you. We must understand that it is only in the day of **Yeshua/Jesus** on earth that we can receive help from Jehovah/Yahweh the Father. The day of the LORD is also the day of **Yeshua/Jesus** because Yeshua is the visible **LORD/Jehovah/Yahweh** of the invisible Father Yahweh/Jehovah.

"Lift up your eyes to the heavens, and look upon the earth beneath: for the heavens shall vanish away like smoke, and the earth shall wax as a garment, and they that dwell therein shall die in like manner: but my salvation shall be forever, and my righteousness shall not be abolished forever" (Isaiah 51:6). *Interpretation: Lift up your eyes to the heavens, and look upon the earth beneath. For the earth shall vanish away as smoke; and the earth shall wax old as a garment, but **my *Yeshua/Jesus*** shall be forever and my ***"righteousness"*** (Tzaddik) shall not be abolished.

"For the moth shall eat them up like wool: but my righteousness shall be forever and my salvation from generation to generation" (Isaiah 51:8). *Interpretation: For the moth shall eat them up like a garment, and the worm shall eat them like wool: but my righteousness (Tzaddik) shall be forever and my **Yeshua/Jesus** from generation to generation.

Please kindly take note of this: The word **"Tzaddik"** can be found in Psalm 119:137. It is the eighteenth alphabet in Psalm 119 and the encoded sign of the Messiah. The blessed and beloved Son of our heavenly Father is both His Salvation (**Yeshua**) and Righteousness (**Tzaddik**). For further insight on this, let us read Matthew 6:33, *"But seek ye first the kingdom of God, and his righteousness; and all these things shall be added unto you."*

*Interpretation: But seek you first the Kingdom (Government) of God and His Tzaddik (Righteousness) and all these shall be added unto you.

"How good upon the mountain are the feet of him that bringeth good tidings, that publisheth peace; that bringeth good tidings of good, that publisheth salvation; that saith unto Zion, Thy God reigneth!" (Isaiah 52:9).
*Interpretation: How beautiful upon the mountain are the feet of him that brings good tidings, who publishes peace, who brings good news of good, and that

publishes **"Yeshua/Jesus."** That says unto Zion, Your God reigns! The very God of Zion is the **'Salvation/Yeshua/Jesus of Nazareth/Israel.'**

"The LORD hath made bare his holy arm in the eyes of all the nations; and all the ends of the earth shall see the salvation of our God" (Isaiah 52:10).
*Interpretation: Yahweh/Jehovah the Father has made bare His holy arm in the eyes of all the nations and all the ends of the earth shall see **Yeshua/Jesus** of our God. As **Yeshua/Jesus of Nazareth/Israel** walked on earth, all the ends of the earth saw Him and His glory. It was during the reign of the Roman Empire that the **Salvation/Yeshua/Jesus** of our God was born on earth and the entire world saw Him in Galilee, Judah, Jerusalem, and all the land of Israel and on the Cross of Calvary.

"Thus saith the LORD, keep you judgment and do justice: for my salvation is near to come; and my righteousness to be revealed" (Isaiah 56:1, Emphasis mine).
*Interpretation: Thus says the Holy Spirit, keep and maintain judgment and justice for yourselves: because my **Yeshua/Jesus** is near to come; and my ***Tzaddik*** to be revealed. Today, the **Everlasting Yeshua/Jesus** of God has come near to all. The **Yeshua/Jesus** of our God is also the Yeshua of Israel.

"And he saw that there was no man, and wondered that there was no intercessor: therefore his arm brought salvation unto him, and his righteousness it sustained him" (Isaiah 59:16, Emphasis mine).
*Interpretation: And He (The Father) saw that there was no man and wondered that there was no intercessor: therefore, His arm brought **Yeshua** to Him and **His Tzaddik**, it sustained Him.

"Violence shall no more be heard in thy land, wasting nor destruction within thy borders; but thou shalt call thy walls salvation and thy gates praise" (Isaiah 60:18, Emphasis mine).
*Interpretation/Application: Violence shall no more be heard in thy land, wasting nor destruction within thy borders; but you shall call your walls **Yeshua/Jesus** and your gates praise.

"I will greatly rejoice in the LORD, my soul shall be joyful in my God; for he hath clothed me with the garment of salvation, he hath covered me with the robe of righteousness, as a bridegroom decketh himself with ornament and as a bride adorneth herself with Jewels" (Isaiah 61:10, Emphasis mine).

*Interpretation: I will greatly rejoice in Jehovah, my soul shall be joyful in my God; for He has clothed me with the garments of **Yeshua/Jesus** and has covered me with robe of Tzaddik as a bridegroom decks himself and as a bride adorns herself with jewels.

"For Zion's sake will I not hold my peace, and for Jerusalem's sake I will not rest, until the righteousness thereof go forth as brightness, and the salvation thereof as a lamp that burneth" [Isaiah 62:1]
*Interpretation: For Zion's sake, I will not hold my peace, and for Jerusalem's sake, I will not rest until the **Tzaddik** thereof go forth as brightness and the **Yeshua/Jesus** thereof as a lamp that burns.

"Behold, the LORD hath proclaimed unto the end of the world, Say ye to the daughter of Zion, Behold, thy salvation cometh; behold, his reward is with him; and his work before him" (Isaiah 62:11).
*Interpretation: Behold Jehovah has proclaimed unto the end of the world, say you to Zion, behold, your ***Yeshua/Jesus*** comes. Behold His reward is with Him and His work before Him.

THE GRANDEST PLAN OF GOD FOR ALL NATIONS

The greatest and grandest plan of God the Father through the Holy Ghost is for all flesh or people in all the nations of the earth to see the **Salvation/Yeshua** of God. This all-important plan was revealed to Isaiah and John the Baptist respectively in different generations. The purposed revelation of **Yeshua/Jesus** to all flesh is the ***'nucleuses'*** of revelations in the

entire Bible. Now listen to the prophecy of Isaiah according to chapter 40:5... *"And the glory of the LORD shall be revealed, and all flesh shall see it together: for the mouth of the LORD has spoken it."* Here the word **'it'** means the **Salvation/Yeshua of Israel.** A deep study shows that *there is a divine correlation between the book of Isaiah and book of Luke.*

The inseparable mystery in both books *is that the* ***'glory'*** *of God in Isaiah 40:5 is called the* ***'salvation'*** *of God in Luke 3:6 as thus, "And all flesh shall see the salvation of God."* Therefore, the **glory** of God equals the **'Salvation/Yeshua'** of God.

Furthermore, the **glory of God**, which is also equal to **the glory of Israel,** is tantamount to the **Salvation/Yeshua of God**, which equals the **Salvation/Yeshua of Israel.**

In the book of Exodus 24: 16-17 the Bible says, *"And the glory of the LORD abode upon mount Sinai, and the cloud covered it six days: and the seventh day he called unto Moses out of the midst of the cloud. And the sight of the glory of the LORD was like devouring fire on the top of the mount in the eyes of the children of Israel."*

The **Glory/Salvation/Yeshua/Jesus** of Father Yahweh who is equally the **Glory/Salvation/Yeshua/Jesus** of Israel was the grandest revelation of the Holy Ghost to the children of Israel immediately they came out of Egypt. The Holy Ghost gathered all the children of Israel upon Mount Sinai for them to see the **Glory/Salvation/Yeshua** of their father Israel. In that spiritual state in which He appeared to them, the **Salvation/Yeshua/Jesus** was in the sight of the children of Israel as devouring fire.

However, in His corporeal state when He appeared to be the last sacrificial Lamb of atonement that takes away the sin of the world, He emptied Himself of His nature of devouring fire and became as an ordinary man. *"Who, being in the form of God, thought it not robbery to be equal with God: But made himself of no reputation, and took upon him the form of a servant, and was made in the likeness of men: And being found in the fashion as a man, he humbled himself, and became obedient unto death, even the death of the cross"*
(Philippians 2:6-8).

For deeper insight on this let us read Lamentation 3:26 "It is good that a man should hope and quietly wait for the salvation of the LORD."

Prophet Jeremiah who was an ardent exponent of the promised Salvation of Israel said to his fellow Jewish people that it is good that a man *hopes* and *quietly waits* for the **Salvation/Yeshua/Jesus** of the LORD just as their father Israel also did according to Genesis 49:18. Please consider this table below for proper balancing of the Scriptures.

Isaiah 40:5	Luke 3:6
"And the glory of the LORD shall be revealed, and all flesh shall see it together: for the mouth of the LORD hath spoken it."	*"And all flesh shall see the salvation of God."*

The grandest purpose of God Almighty is for all flesh (Jews and Gentiles, Black and White people, and all races on earth) to see the 'Glory/Salvation/Yeshua/Jesus' of God together. This grandest plan ever resounds in the heart of the Holy Ghost as thus..."And the Glory/Salvation/Yeshua/Jesus of God shall be revealed and all flesh/people shall see Him because the mouth of the LORD has spoken it. However, we are called to pull down every high thing that exalts itself against the knowledge of God or the revelation of Yeshua/Jesus to all flesh. Satan has blinded the eyes of people so that they will not see the 'Glory/Salvation of God.' In these last days, Satan and his demons must be cast down to the pit so that all flesh will see Yeshua/Jesus of Israel/Nazareth according to **God's original grandest plans.**

THE DELIVERANCE OF PROPHET JONAH BY THE SALVATION/YESHUA/JESUS OF ISRAEL

All the prophets in Israel had personal encounters with the Salvation/Yeshua of Israel. Each one of those prophets worshipped and served Yeshua/Jesus of Israel. Jonah said in Chapter 2:9, *"But I will sacrifice* In verse 10 of Jonah 2, Yahweh/Jehovah of Israel who became Salvation/Yeshua/Jesus to all the prophets as well as individual persons in Israel spoke to the fish that swallowed up Jonah and it vomited him out upon the dry land. Indeed, Yeshua/Jesus of Israel/Nazareth is the only Saviour of all men. Both the raging sea, tumultuous wind, the great fish in the sea, the grave and death hear and obey His voice only. He is the only 'Ruler' in Israel whose voice alone saves all the Israelites from their troubles.

CHAPTER 8

JESUS AND ZACCHEUS

"And Jesus said unto him, this day is salvation come into this house for as much as he also is a son of Abraham" (Luke 19:9, Emphasis mine).

*Here, the Person and the Man whose name is **Yeshua** came into the house of Zaccheus to dine with him. This statement, *"This day is salvation come into this house"* means, this day is **Yeshua/Jesus** come into your house, Zaccheus. All the Jews must open their houses to the **Salvation/Yeshua/Jesus of Israel/Nazareth** to come in.

JESUS AND THE JEWS

"Ye worship ye know not what: we know what we worship: for salvation is of the Jews" (John 4:22)...*"For salvation is of the Jews"* means for **"Yeshua/ Jesus"** is of the Jews.

THE TRUE MEANING OF JESUS OF NAZARETH

The true meaning of Jesus of Nazareth is also the same as **Yeshua of Nazareth.** He can also be called the **Salvation** of Nazareth. Demons affirm this axiomatically, *"Saying, Let us alone; what have we to do with thee, thou Jesus of Nazareth? Art thou come to destroy us? I know who thou art, the Holy One of God"* (Luke 4:34).

Even the unclean spirits call the beloved Son of God, Jesus of Nazareth. Those demons confess veraciously that they know who He is—the Holy One of God. This very **Jesus/Yeshua** of Nazareth or the **Salvation of Nazareth** encoded in the Old Testament by this code **Salvation** is the same Person that the Scriptures refer to as the Holy One of Israel. *"I am the LORD, your Holy one, the creator of Israel your king"* (Isaiah 43:15).

"For I am the LORD thy God, the Holy One of Israel, thy Savior: I gave Egypt for thy ransom, Ethiopia and Seba for thee" (Isaiah 43:3)... "I am the LORD, your Holy One, the creator of Israel, your King" (Isaiah 43: 15).

Therefore, those unclean spirits referred and still refer to **Yeshua of Israel/Nazareth** as the Holy One of God as well as the Holy One of Israel. In Israel, there was a city called Galilee. Nazareth is a sub-city in Galilee in which all the Nazarites of God got their revelation and education on the **'Coming Salvation'** of Israel. Those Nazarites had their primary and higher education on the ***'Coming One'*** whose name would be called **"Yeshua/Jesus"** that would deliver them from their troubles and sins.

Among the Nazarites of Nazareth were men like Samuel, Samson, David, Isaiah, Jeremiah, Habakkuk and many others. Each one of them fought for the deliverance of the children of Israel from their enemies by pointing them to the **Salvation/Yeshua of Israel**. As each one of them was about dying, the promise that God made unto Israel their father, was re-affirmed to them — "wait for **Yeshua/Jesus of Israel** who will save the city of Nazareth, Judah, Jerusalem, Israel and the whole world.

"And the LORD spake unto Moses saying, Speak unto the children of Israel, and say unto them, When either man or woman shall separate themselves, to vow a vow of a Nazarite, to separate themselves unto the LORD: He shall separate himself from wine and strong drink and shall drink no vinegar of wine, or vinegar of strong drink, neither shall he drink any liquor of grapes nor eat moist grapes, or dried" (Numbers 6:1-3). *"And he came and dwelt in a city called Nazareth: that it might be fulfilled which was spoken by prophets, he shall be called a Nazarene"* (Matthew 2:23).

Our King and the everlasting Father the Lord Yeshua came and dwelt in the city of Nazareth when they had come back to Israel from the land of Egypt so that He shall be called a ***'Nazarene'*** or **"Tsemach."** Yeshua of Nazareth is therefore, the ***Nazarene*** of Nazareth. In a deeper sense of approach and application to this truth, He is the **Nazarene of the Nazarites of Nazareth.**

He saves cities and the inhabitants thereof. He ever lives to save the cities of Nazareth, Judah, Jerusalem, Israel, and all the cities of the world from Satan and his evil angels. All the prophets according to Matthew 2:23 prophesied that Yeshua of Israel would dwell in the city of Nazareth so that He might be called **the Nazarene.** *"To him give all the prophets witness, that through his name whosoever believeth in him shall receive remission of sins"* (Acts 10:43).

Therefore, the name **'Nazarene'** denotes the **'Holy One'** of God, which is also further referred to as the "**Holy One"** of Israel. He is also the righteous One [**Tzaddik**] of both God and Israel. In skipping to Habakkuk, we have the greatest demonstration of the Name **"JESUS"** in the Old Testament. From here, we have the name as well as the title of the Saviour. In Habakkuk 3:13, we read literally from the original Hebrew: *"Thou wentest forth with thy Yeshua/Jesus of [or for] thy people: with Yeshua thy Messiah (thine Anointed One i.e. with Jesus thy Anointed) thou woundest the head of the house of the wicked one [Satan]."*

Here, we have the full blossom of the very **'Name'** given to our LORD in the New Testament —JESUS CHRIST! So, do not let anyone Jew or Gentile tell you that the name of **Jesus** is not found in the Old Testament/Hebrew Scripture. And as aged Simeon came to the temple, being led there by the Holy Spirit, and took the baby **'Yeshua'** in his arms, he said, *"Lord, now lettest thou thy servant depart in peace, according to thy word: for mine eyes have seen thy Salvation/Yeshua /Jesus* (Luke 2:29-30).

Certainly, not only did his eyes see God's **Salvation/Yeshua/Jesus** but he also felt and touched Him. His believing heart beat with joy and assurance as he felt the loving heart of God throbbing in the heart of the Holy infant, Yeshua/Jesus.

*"And thou shall call his name Jesus (**Salvation/Yeshua**); for he shall save (salvage) his people from their sins."* ***For details on His blueprint for our redemption, see Isaiah 53:1-12.***

THE DEITY OF YESHUA/JESUS OF NAZARETH

The authority of the Scriptures and the detailed treatise on this piece of work agree explicitly on the 'deity' of our Lord Jesus. Our Saviour Jesus Christ is the very Yahweh/Jehovah revealed in the Old Testament. Part of our vision for this book is that the Holy Spirit will use it to destroy the deep-seated darkness in the minds of Islamic Community who are averse to the 'deity' of our Lord Jesus. In Surah 5:116 of the Islamic Qur'an, our Lord Jesus is presented by Muhammad as receiving query from Allah for allowing people to regard Him and His mother as gods. Since the authority of the Holy Scriptures is infallible, all the Jewish prophets and apostles by the authenticity and irrevocability of both the Old and New Testaments firmly declare that **Yeshua/Jesus** of Nazareth is the very Almighty God of Abraham, Isaac and Israel.

Only our Lord **Yeshua/Jesus** is to be worshipped by all. Nevertheless, Mary is not a deity at all and she should not be deified, prayed through or called upon for anything. All the Jews that were followers of **Jesus/Yeshua** only worshipped Him and not Mary. They did not worship Mary for any reason. The Roman Catholic Christians deified and introduced the worship of Mary who was only a human vessel through whom our Lord was born on earth. Mary is not the queen of heaven that the Roman Catholics claim she is.

This assertion to queen of heaven is found in Jeremiah chapters 7:18 and 44:18-19, 25. The issue of queen of heaven has been before Mary was born. Therefore, how can she be the queen of heaven and queen of all the angels? To our Orthodox Jews and the entire Islamic world, Yahweh/Jehovah has truly become our **Yeshua/Jesus** as was revealed to Moses, the prophet, and David, the King of Israel, and other prophets.

FULL TREATISE ON THE RIGHTEOUS BRANCH

When we say that the **'Salvation/Yeshua/Jesus of Israel'** is also Yahweh/Jehovah, we need to understand the Biblical structure of the divine assertion. A proper knowledge of the ***'Branch or Tsemach or Nazarene of Righteousness,'*** will resolve the confusion in the churches, among Orthodox Jews and the world at large. Meanwhile, the book of Jeremiah sternly and absolutely resolved this issue. *"Behold, the days come, saith the LORD, that I* *will raise unto David a righteous Branch, and a King shall reign and prosper, and shall execute judgment and justice in the earth. In his days Judah shall be saved, and Israel shall dwell safely: and this is his name whereby he shall be called, THE LORD (YAHWEH) OUR RIGHTEOUSNESS" (Jeremiah 23:5-6).*

In the above Scripture, we need to break down the promise of Yahweh/Jehovah the Father to David and Jerusalem: ➢ *"I will raise unto David a Righteous Branch,"*

- *"And a Righteous King shall reign and prosper,"*
- *"The Righteous Branch and King shall execute judgment and justice on earth,"*
- *"In the days of the Righteous Branch and King that reigns and prospers shall Judah be saved,"*
- *"In the days of the Righteous Branch and King that reigns and prospers shall Israel dwell safely,"*
- *"And this is His name whereby He (the Righteous Branch and King) shall be called,* ***'THE LORD/YAHWEH/JEHOVAH OUR RIGHTEOUSNESS.' "***

In this Scripture above, Yahweh/Jehovah the supreme Father revealed to Jeremiah the personal name of His own and only begotten Son that would come to save Judah and make Israel dwell in safety. By the Scriptures of the prophets, Yahweh the Father commands all the children of Israel and the whole world to call the '*Righteous Branch and King* that prospers and reigns who is His Very Son, the exact name that He the Supreme Father has given Him. Therefore, the proper name of the very *'Righteous Branch and King' that* the Father by His Spirit has raised unto David that saves Judah and grants security to Israel is called in English language ***'THE LORD OUR RIGHTEOUSNESS,'*** and in Hebrew language, ***'YAHWEH/JEHOVAH TZIDKENU.'***

The table below shows the relational bond that exists in the Great White Throne of Heaven. Our Father in heaven shares the same *'Throne, Name, Power, Spirit, Glory, Kingdom, Word,'* etc, with His only begotten Son who is the ***'Salvation/Yeshua/Jesus of Israel.'*** In the four gospels clinically reported by Matthew, Mark Luke and John, ***'Yeshua/Jesus of Israel/Nazareth'*** called the very God in heaven that sent Him into the world, *'My Father.'* However, in Isaiah 9:6, our Father in heaven decreed that His Son's name should be called,

'The Everlasting Father.' This is a mysterious relational bond between the Father and His Son.

However, the Holy Ghost has also provided the Scriptural tools for unlocking the mystery of the *Righteous Branch and King.* In dealing with this high-topic, we are going to use the keys of the kingdom hidden in Zechariah 6:12, *"And speak unto him, saying, Thus speaketh the LORD of hosts, saying, Behold the man whose name is The BRANCH; and he shall build the temple of the LORD."* Please consider these phrases: *the Son of God, the Branch of Righteousness, the Prince of Peace, etc.* Here Yahweh/Jehovah the Father repeats what He said to Jeremiah to Zechariah.

Yahweh/Jehovah the Father said to Zechariah by His Spirit, behold the *'Man whose name is the Branch.'* All the prophets in Israel knew about the Man whose name is the '*Righteous Branch and King.* They all knew that He would be the Son of Yahweh the Father and that He would come to save Judah, Jerusalem, Israel and the entire world from Satan the adversary of all men. They all read the books of Jeremiah and others just as Daniel did. From the book of Jeremiah, they all knew that Yahweh the Father by His Holy Spirit commanded all men everywhere to call the man whose name is the Righteous Branch and King—**Yahweh/Jehovah Tzidkenu.**

Contemporarily, a branch of a 'head office' bears the same name structure with the parent office. The branch of First Bank for example in Abuja, the capital city of Nigeria bears the same brand name of First Bank in Kaduna, Lagos, Abia states, etc. A branch of 'Shell oil and Gas Company' whose 'head office' is in the U. S. A, shares the same brand name with the parent body overseas. I can go on and on and give elaborate examples of parent establishments and their branches but sufficient are the few examples above. In 1Corinthians 11:3, the Bible tells us that Yahweh/Jehovah/God the Father is the "head" of the Messiah/Christ.

Therefore, since Yahweh/Jehovah/God the Father is the head of the Messiah/Christ, who is the **Salvation/Yeshua/Jesus of Israel**, it means that **Yeshua/Jesus** is His sole and only Branch. Please understand that **Yeshua/Jesus of Israel** is the same **Yeshua/Jesus of Nazareth**. Below are some random samples authenticating the divine and inseparable bond between Yahweh/Jehovah/God the Father and His Son who is called Yahweh/Jehovah/God the Son.

1	**Yahweh/Jehovah /God**	**Branch of Yahweh/Jehovah**	**Yeshua/Jesus the Messiah is the Man whose name is Yahweh/Jehovah/God.**
2	**Righteousness**	**Branch of Righteousness**	**Yeshua/Jesus the Messiah is the Man whose name is Righteousness.**
3	**Peace (In Isaiah 9:6, The Father is Peace whereas the Son is Prince, hence, *'the Prince of Peace).'***	**Branch of Peace**	**Yeshua/Jesus the Messiah is the Man whose name is Peace... Micah 5:5; Ephesians 2:14.**
4	**Holy and Reverend (Ps.111:9), In John 17:11a the Son addresses the Father thus, *'Holy Father...'***	**Branch of the Holy and Reverend Father**	**Yeshua/Jesus the Messiah is the Man whose name is Holy and Reverend... Remember that all the devils call Him the 'Holy One of God'... Luke 4: 34.**

5	Power (Matthew 26:64)	Branch of Power	Yeshua/Jesus the Messiah is the Man whose name is the Power of God…1Corinthians 1:24.
6	Glory	Branch of Glory	Yeshua/Jesus the Messiah is the Man whose name is Glory in heaven and earth.
7	Majesty on High (Hebrews 1:3; 8:1)	Branch of the Majesty on High	Yeshua/Jesus the Messiah is the Man whose name is Majesty in heaven and earth.
8	Father in heaven	Branch of the Father in heaven	Yeshua/Jesus the Messiah is the Man whose name is the everlasting Father.
9	The Mountain (Daniel 2:45)	Branch of the Mountain… Please take note of this, the 'Stone' from the 'Mountain' became a 'great Mountain 'and filled the whole earth … Daniel 2: 35).	Yeshua/Jesus the Messiah is the Man whose name is the 'Great Mountain.' He is the same Rock/Mountain that followed the children of Israel as they wandered in the wilderness… 1Corithians 10:4.

10	**Most High**	**Branch of the Most High**	**Yeshua/ Jesus the Messiah is the Man whose name is the Most High.**
11	**Almighty God**	**Branch of the Almighty God**	**Yeshua/Jesus the Messiah is the Man whose name is the Almighty God.**
12	**Ancient of days**	**Branch of the Ancient of days**	**Yeshua/Jesus the Messiah is the Man whose name is the Ancient of days.**
13	**"But he held his peace and answered nothing. Again the high priest asked him, and said unto him, Art thou the Christ, the Son of the Blessed? And Jesus said, I am..." (Mark 14:61-62). The Father's name is the 'BLESSED'**	**"Blessed be he that cometh in the name of the LORD: we have blessed you out of the house of the LORD" (Psalm 118:26). Our Lord Jesus is the Branch of the 'BLESSED'**	**Yeshua/Jesus the Messiah is the Man whose name is the BLESSED. He is the 'visible Blessed Son of the invisible Blessed Father**

"Who is the image of the invisible God, the first born of every creature" (Colossians 1:15) ... *"No man hath seen God at any time: the only begotten Son, which is in the bosom of the Father, he hath declared him"* (John 1:18). From Adam to Abraham and down to Moses and all the prophets, no man had at any time seen Yahweh/Jehovah the Father who is the invisible God. The only Person that each one of them saw is the only begotten Son who is the visible God of the invisible God. The Son is the very visible Yahweh/Jehovah whom Moses saw in the burning bush. The invisible Father Yahweh sent Him. He is the only one who is in the bosom of the Father. He is the Father's direct emissary to all men in all generations. He has been appearing to humanity to declare His Father to them for the purpose of adoption unto election.

DIVINE LAWS OF REPRODUCTION

In the book of Genesis, Yahweh/Jehovah the all-wise God instituted the laws of re-production for every living thing He created. *"And God said, Let the earth bring forth living creature after his kind, cattle, and creeping thing, and beast of the earth after his kind: and it was so. And God made the beast of the earth after his kind and cattle after his kind, and everything that creepeth upon the earth after his kind: and God saw that it was good"* (Genesis 1:24-25).

The instituted law of '*bringing forth or coming forth from*' applies to both God, man, animals, birds, trees, fishes and all living creatures. Naturally, a father '*brings forth*' a son or daughter. Consequently, a son or daughter 'comes forth' from a father. By these divinely instituted laws of reproduction of same species, man brings forth man-kind, trees bring forth tree-kind, animals bring forth animal-kind, fishes bring forth fish-kind, and so forth according to the power that God has given them. This same standard of '*bringing forth*' one's kind applies also to Yahweh/Jehovah the Father who has an inherent power within Himself to bring forth or reproduce a Son of His own kind known as Yahweh the Son—Jesus of Nazareth the only true Messiah.

Our Lord Jesus further authenticates the veracious claims of 'coming forth or bringing forth from' in the book of John. *"I came forth from the Father, and am come into the world: again, I leave the world and go to the Father"* (John 16:28, Emphasis mine). This Scripture shows that our Lord Jesus is

Yahweh-kind because He *'came forth'* from Yahweh the Father. In Hebrews 1:3, our Lord Jesus who is Yahweh/Jehovah-kind is addressed by Apostle Paul as the express image of His Person i.e. the Person of Yahweh the Father. Our Lord Jesus *'came forth from'* the Father because Yahweh the Father *'brought Him forth.'* For this very reason, He is called the **Branch** of Yahweh.

Consequently, the **Branch** or 'Offshoot' of Yahweh the Father is Yahweh the Son. In the book of Mark 14:61-62, when Caiaphas asked our Lord Jesus, *"Are you the Christ, the Son of the Blessed?"* Our Lord Jesus answered and said to him, *"I AM..."* The emphatic, the metaphoric and the unwavering answer that Yahweh the Son gave to Caiaphas led the high priest to rend his priestly clothes. By this act, Caiaphas the priest violated the divine order of Leviticus 10:6, thereby terminating forever the priestly order of Levi before Christ Jesus who is the 'High Priest forever after the order of Melchizedek.' Yahweh/Jehovah the Father who is called the *'Blessed'* by the ancient Hebrews *'brought forth'* a Son whose name is the *'Branch of the Blessed.'*

The visible *'BRANCH/Son'* that *came forth from* the 'Blessed Invisible Father' is unequivocally the *'Blessed Visible One'* of Israel because He has been *brought forth* by Yahweh/Jehovah the 'Blessed Father' who is invisible. Our Messiah Yeshua/Jesus is the very Man revealed in Psalm 118:26. He is the Man unto whom the generation of King David said, **'Blessed is HE** that cometh in the name of Yahweh/Jehovah/the LORD". He has come indeed as the Bible foretold. If we are going to please the Holy Ghost in this perverse and adulterous generation, we must join the generation of King David and say, *'Blessed be Yahweh/Jehovah who has become our Yeshua/Jesus, the Branch of Father Yahweh who came forth from Yahweh the Father into the world for our redemption.' We have blessed you oh Yahweh/Jehovah/the Lord Yeshua/Jesus of Israel/Nazareth out of our hearts and churches.*

From the 'Righteous Father' came forth the 'Righteous Son.' From the 'Glorious Father' came forth the 'Glorious Son.' From the 'Living Father' came forth the 'Living Son.' From the 'Ancient Father' came forth the 'Ancient Son.' From the 'Majestic Father' came forth the 'Majestic Son.' From the 'Dreaded Mountain' of Daniel 2:45, came forth the 'Dreaded Stone' that became a 'Great Mountain which fills the earth according to Daniel 2:35.

The instituted law of 'bringing forth or coming forth from' applies to both God, man, animals, birds, trees, fishes and all living creatures. Naturally, a father 'brings forth' a son or daughter. Consequently, a son or daughter 'comes forth' from a father. By these divinely instituted laws of reproduction of same species, man brings forth man-kind, trees bring forth tree-kind, animals bring forth animal-kind, fishes bring forth fish-kind, and so forth according to the power that God has given them. This same standard of 'bringing forth' one's kind applies also to Yahweh/Jehovah the Father who has an inherent power within Himself to bring forth or reproduce a Son of His own kind known as Yahweh the Son—Jesus of Nazareth the only true Messiah.

Our Lord Jesus further authenticates the veracious claims of 'coming forth or bringing forth from' in the book of John. “I came forth from the Father, and am come into the world: again, I leave the world and go to the Father” (John 16:28, Emphasis mine). This Scripture shows that our Lord Jesus is Yahweh-kind because He 'came forth' from Yahweh the Father.

From Adam to Moses and the rest of the saints, none of them saw Yahweh/Jehovah the Father. Nevertheless, the Person that appeared to them is rather the **'Righteous Branch/Tzemach'** whose name is Yahweh/Jehovah/the LORD **Yeshua/Jesus of Israel/Nazareth.** When Yeshua/Jesus of Israel appeared to Moses, He declared His proper name to Moses. He said to Moses, *'I am Yahweh/Jehovah.'* He said that this is His name and memorial in all generations. Therefore, on this premise, we boldly call our Saviour who is the Lamb of God, *“Yahweh Yeshua of Israel our Messiah Jehovah Jesus our Messiah The Lord Jesus our Messiah.*

In the New Testament, the Greek the word “Kurios” translated “Lord” in English language is finessed in Hebrew language “YHWH or Yahweh.”
Therefore, when we say that the **Salvation/Yeshua/Jesus of Israel/Nazareth** is **'Kurios'**, its crystal meaning is that the ***'Salvation/ Yeshua/Jesus of Israel'*** is **'Yahweh.'** All traditional Judaism must embrace and adhere to this truth set forth in this and other books which have been authenticated by the Scriptures of the prophets of Israel deeply rooted in truth. All forms of traditional Judaism have no excuses whatsoever to argue against this known fact.

The Father's ultimate plan for all Jews and Gentiles according to Philippians 2:10-11 is for all tongues to acknowledge that the ***'Salvation/Yeshua/Jesus of Israel/Nazareth who is the Righteous Branch and King that saves Judah, Israel and***

the world', is ***'Kurios'*** or ***'Yahweh'*** to the glory of the Father. In heaven, all the tongues of angels are confessing that Yeshua/Jesus the Messiah is Yahweh/Jehovah. Beneath the earth, all the tongues of both Lucifer and his doomed demons confess that Yeshua of Israel is Kurios/Yahweh.

THE IRREVOCABLE VERACITY AND PROOF THAT YESHUA/JESUS IS YAHWEH/JEHOVAH

Please carefully study this table below for comparative analysis. As you follow the revealed Word of God, you will be amazed by the Scriptural consensus on this matter. The authority of the Scriptures resolves every debate and challenge perfectly. Two prophets of Israel namely Micah and Habakkuk who also waited for the coming of the **Salvation/Yeshua/Jesus of Israel/Nazareth,** were metaphorical about the very truth that Yeshua/Jesus is Himself Yahweh/Jehovah.

Micah 5:2	Habakkuk 1:12
"But thou, Bethlehem Ephratah, though thou be little among the thousands of Judah, yet out of thee shall he come forth unto me that is to be ruler in Israel; whose goings forth have been from of old, from everlasting (Emphasis mine)."	***"Art thou not from everlasting,*** **O LORD** ***(YAHWEH/JEHOVAH) myGod, mine Holy One? We shall not die O LORD (YAHWEH/JEHOVAH), thou hast ordained them for judgment: O mighty God thou hast established them for correction (Emphasis mine)."***

The prophecy of Micah reveals to us that out of Bethlehem in Ephratah would come a **ruler** in Israel whose goings forth have been from of old, even from everlasting. Then, Habakkuk the prophet by the Holy Spirit said in the above Scripture, *"Art thou not from everlasting, O LORD/YAHWEH/JEHOVAH, mine Holy One?"* Here prophet Habakkuk who read the prophecies of prophets Jeremiah, Micah and other prophets that prophesied about the **'Coming Ruler'** in Israel, also prayed to that **'Coming Ruler'** and said, *"Art thou not from everlasting, O LORD/YAHWEH/JEHOVAH, mine Holy One?*

Comparatively and metaphorically, Micah 5:2 says ***from everlasting***... Then Habakkuk 1:12 says ***from everlasting.*** In the time of the ancient Israelites, their God through prophet Moses established an unchanging standard for perfect judgment and rulings. *"One witness shall not rise up against a man for any iniquity, or for any sin, in any sin that he sinneth: at the mouth of two witnesses, or at the mouth of three witnesses, shall the matter be established"* **(Deuteronomy 19:15)**. Our only and true Master Jesus of Israel/Nazareth who is the Messiah also confirmed this divine order in Matthew 18:16, *"But if he will not hear thee, then take with thee one or two more, that in the mouth of two or three witnesses every word may be established."* Apostle Paul also said, *"This is the third time I am coming to you. In the mouth of two or three witnesses shall every word be established"* (2Corinthians 13:1).

The consensus veracity and conformity of Micah 5:2 and Habakkuk 1:12 based on the above Scriptural rulings for judgment, show without controversy that Micah, Habakkuk, and others were witnesses who heaven and the Israelites confirmed to be genuine prophets. Through their prophecies it has been established through their mouths that the **Salvation/Yeshua/Jesus of Israel/Nazareth** who was born in Bethlehem –Ephratah to be the Ruler/King in Israel, who is *from everlasting*, is therefore ipso facto **'Yahweh/Jehovah'** according to the Hebrew Scriptures written by all the Hebrew prophets.

However, on earth only the tongues of Orthodox Jews and those deceived through traditional Judaism apparently are confessing the opposite. Let it be known to all the Jews and the whole world that **Yeshua/Jesus of Israel/ Nazareth** who was born in Bethlehem Ephrathah in the days of King Herod, Pontius Pilate, Caiaphas and Anas, is the only true Messiah and the very Yahweh/Jehovah they read about in their Hebrew Scriptures and have been waiting for. He is ipso facto the only "Hope" of the world and the Jews.

Any other *'Messiah/Christ'* other than **Yeshua/Jesus of Israel/Nazareth who is Yahweh the Son** that the Jews are waiting for will definitely be a false Messiah and Satan in disguise. Let all the Jews and the whole world beware and heed this warning! Any Jew or Gentile that rejects this very Messiah who is **Yeshua/Jesus of Israel /Nazareth our blessed Yahweh the Branch** of the invisible Yahweh the Father, will face the wrath of Yahweh the Father in hell fire. All Jews must beware of a *'mendacious Messiah'* that opposes the *'veracious Messiah'* of the Jews and the whole world who is ***Yahweh/Jehovah Yeshua/Jesus of Israel/Nazareth.*** We conclude therefore that any Jew who would claim to be the *'Messiah'* is actually saying that he is Yahweh/Jehovah.

CHAPTER 9

THE WATCH TOWER SOCIETY (JEHOVAH'S WITNESS) AND JESUS

For many years, 'Jehovah's Witness group' have injected confusion and canard into the minds of Christians and non- Christians with their anti-Christ teachings. With their unbending orthodoxy, they have initiated a subtle but conscientious war against the Person of our Lord Jesus Christ. In my work of evangelism, I have met several Jehovah's Witness members. However, the very experience and challenge that led me to do more investigative and intensive readings and studies of the Bible was when I met one of their women for Bible discussion. As we discussed the Person of our Saviour, I referred her to Isaiah 9:6c where the Bible says that the 'Child' that is born unto us and the 'Son' that is given to us shall be called the 'Mighty God' (El-Gibbor), she admitted it without hesitation. Nevertheless, she said and I quote her, 'there is no place where Jesus is called the "Almighty God" in the entire Bible.

The first challenge I had was when one of them told me that there is no place where the name 'Jesus' can be seen in the Old Testament. The Watch Tower members allege that Jesus is not Jehovah. In their own Bible, they also teach that Jesus is a **'god'** and not **'God.'**

YESHUA/JESUS OF NAZARETH IS THE ALMIGHTY/THE MIGHTY GOD

Since the Bible is *'the Absolute and Final Authority'* for both angels, demons and human beings, we will also rely on the immutable veracity of the same in dealing with the mendacious doctrines of Jehovah's Witness aimed at turning people away from the ancient and true Light of Israel and of the world—Yeshua/Jesus. Here we will be comparing Scripture with Scripture. Please study this chart.

ISAIAH 9:6	ISAIAH 10:20-21	JEREMIAH 32:18-19
"For unto us a child is born, and unto us a son is given: and the government shall be upon his shoulder: and his name shall be called wonderful, Counsellor, The mighty God, the everlasting Father, the Prince of Peace"	***" And it shall come to pass in that day, that the remnant of Israel, and such as are escaped of the house of Jacob, shall no more again stay upon him that smote them; but shall stay upon the LORD, the Holy One of Israel, in truth. The remnant will return even the remnant of Jacob, unto the mighty God"***	***"Thou shewest loving kindness unto thousands, and recompensest the iniquity of the fathers into the bosom of their children after them: the Great, the Mighty God, the LORD of hosts, is his name, great in counsel, and mighty in work: for thine eyes are open upon the sons of men: to give everyone according to his ways, and according to the fruit of his doings"***

From all solvable Scriptural indices, another two witnesses that are in agreement with Isaiah 9:6 have emerged which prove that the LORD/Yahweh/Jehovah is called 'The Mighty God' in both Isaiah 10:21 and Jeremiah 32:18-19. Now since the name of the Child and Son of God—Yeshua/Jesus of Nazareth is called the 'Mighty God' in Isaiah 9:6, and Isaiah 10:21 and Jeremiah 32:18-19 metaphorically and axiomatically call Him 'The Great, the Mighty God, the LORD of hosts/Yahweh tzavaot/Jehovah of hosts (Emphasis mine), He is ipso facto the Almighty. In Titus 2:13, Paul writes, *"Looking for that blessed hope, and the glorious appearing of the great God and Saviour Jesus Christ."*

The book of Psalm 68 pictures the great works of the Almighty God who scatters kings, leads captivity captive, and receives gifts for men. The comparative analysis of Psalm 68 with Ephesians 4 shows that the Lord Yeshua/Jesus who alone is the Christ is the Almighty/Mighty God of the Hebrews. In as much as each verse of the Bible speaks of our Lord Yeshua/Jesus, it is then of utmost imperative for us to carry out Biblical equations, checks and balances so that we can solve all problems related to the points we are discussing practically. Please see another chart.

Psalm 68:14 and 18	**Ephesians 4:8-10**
"When the Almighty scattered kings in it, it was white as snow in Salmon"... "Thou hast ascended on high, thou hast led captivity captive: thou hast received gifts for men; yea, for the rebellious also, that the LORD God might dwell among them"	***"Wherefore he saith, When he ascendeth up on high, he led captivity captive, and received gifts unto men. (Now that he ascended, what is it but that he also descended first into the lower parts of the earth? He that descended is the same also that ascended up far above all heavens, that he might fill all things)"***

Since the focus of king David who was the sweet Psalmist in Israel centered on the Almighty God of Abraham, Isaac and Israel, the pronoun *'Thou'* in verse 18 refers to the 'proper name' of the Person of the Almighty in verse 14. Therefore, when we replace the pronoun 'thou' in verse 18 with the noun 'Almighty' in verse 14, we will have:

- The Almighty has ascended on high...
- The Almighty has led captivity captive...
- The Almighty has received gifts for men; yes, for the rebellious also, that the LORD (the Holy Spirit) might dwell among them.

For a deeper understanding of both Psalm 68:14 & 18 and Ephesians 4:8-10, this is the proper setting for comprehensive sentence and application:

- The Almighty Yeshua/Jesus of Israel/Nazareth has ascended on high...

- The Almighty Yeshua/Jesus of Israel/Nazareth has led captivity captive...(*"And the graves were opened; and many bodies of the saints which slept arose, And came out of the graves after his resurrection, and went into the holy city, and appeared unto many"* (Matthew 27:52-53)... *"Thy dead men shall live, together with my dead body shall they arise. Awake and sing ye that dwell in dust: for thy dew is as the dew of the herbs, and the earth shall cast out the dead"* (Isaiah 26:19)).
- The Almighty Yeshua/Jesus of Israel has received gifts for men; yes, for the rebellious also, that the LORD might dwell among them.

Yahweh/Jehovah who alone is the 'Holy One' of Israel, the 'Mighty God' of Israel, the 'Great God' is the very ***'Salvation/Yeshua/Jesus of Israel/Nazareth'***. Between the 'Mighty God' and the 'Almighty God' there is no dichotomy since it refers to One Person—Yeshua/Jesus the Messiah our blessed hope.

These two immutable and uncontroversial Scriptures of Psalm 68 and Ephesians 4 consolidate the proof that Yeshua/Jesus of Israel/Nazareth is *'The Almighty God'* as well as *'The Mighty God.'*

In 1 John 5:20 John wrote, *"And we know that the Son of God is come, and hath given us understanding, that we may know him that is true, and we are in him that is true, even in his Son Jesus Christ. This is the true God, and eternal life."*

Our Lord Jesus is the true God and eternal Life. He is not a 'god' as Charles Taze Russell and all Jehovah's Witness teach. The Watch Tower Bible Society is a false Jehovah's Witness of Jesus. The founder of this movement was a 33rd degree Freemason who hated our Lord Jesus Christ. This hate of our Lord Jesus is common with all the Freemasons. He said in one of his thesis that the Jews are the Messiah/Christ. In his rage against the only Messiah of both the sinful Jews and Gentiles —Yeshua/Jesus of Nazareth, he initiated a Freemasonic movement against the Holy Ghost who glorifies Yahweh/Jehovah the Son on earth. He and other Illuminati/Freemasonic families that hate Yeshua/Jesus of Israel with passion were instrumental in turning the souls of men from the Saviour of all men to Lucifer. Since it has been proved beyond every reasonable doubt that the Salvation/Yeshua/Jesus of Israel is Yahweh/Jehovah, it means that the Jehovah's

Witness have been witnessing against Jesus Christ of Israel/Nazareth who alone is the very God of the Hebrews and the world.

FURTHER IRREVOCABLE PROOFS THAT YESHUA/JESUS IS YAHWEH/JEHOVAH ACCORDING TO THE OLD TESTAMENT

A. JESUS CHRIST THE ANCIENT OF DAYS

Daniel 7:9	Revelation 1:14
"I beheld till the thrones were cast down, and the ancient of days did sit, whose garment is as white as snow, and the hairs of his head like the pure wool: his throne was like the fiery flame, and his wheels like as burning fire"	***"His head and his hairs were white like wool, as white as snow…"***

B. JESUS THE ALL- SEEING YAHWEH/JEHOVAH

Jeremiah 17:10	Revelation 2:23
"I the LORD search the heart, I try the reins, even to give every man according to his ways and according to the fruit of his doing"	***"I will kill her children with death; and all the churches shall know that I am he which searcheth the reins and the hearts: and I will give unto everyone according to your works"***

C. JESUS THE REWARDER OF ALL MEN

Jeremiah 17:10b and 32:19	Revelation 2:23b and 22:12
"Even to give every man according to the fruit of his doing... Great in counsel, and mighty in work: for thine eyes are open upon all the ways of the sons of men: to give everyone according to his ways, and according to the fruit of his doings"	*"And I will give every man according to your works... And , behold I come quickly; and my reward is with me, to give every man according to his work shall be"*

D. YAHWEH/JEHOVAH YESHUA/JESUS THE GOD OF ALL FLESH

Jeremiah 32:27	John 17:3
"Behold, I am the LORD, the God of all flesh: is there anything too hard for me?"	*"As thou hast given him power over all flesh, that he should give eternal life to as many as thou hast given him"*

E. YAHWEH/JEHOVAH YESHUA/JESUS IS THE ALEPH AND TAU (FIRST AND LAST/ALPHA AND OMEGA) WHO DIED FOR ALL MEN

Isaiah 41:4 and 44:6	Revelation 1:17 -18 and 2:8
"Who hath wrought and done it, calling the generations from the beginning? I the LORD, the first, and with the last; I am he"... "Thus saith the LORD the King of Israel, and his redeemer the LORD of hosts; I am the first, and I am the last; and beside me there is no other God"	*"And when I saw him, I fell at his feet as dead. And he laid his right hand upon me, saying unto me, Fear not; I am the first and the last: I am he that liveth, and was dead; and behold I am alive forevermore, Amen; and have the keys of hell and of death"... "And unto the angel of the church in Smyrna write; these things saith the first and the last, which was dead, and is alive"*

F. YAHWEH/JEHOVAH YESHUA/JESUS IS THE ALMIGHTY

Genesis 17:1 and Exodus 6:3	Revelation 4:8, 15:3 and 16:7
"And when Abram was ninety years old and nine the LORD appeared to Abram, and said unto him, I am the Almighty God; walk before me, and be thou perfect"…"And I appeared unto Abraham, unto Isaac, and unto Jacob by the name God Almighty, but by my name JEHOVAH (YAHWEH) was I not known to them" (Emphasis mine).	*"And the four beasts had each of them six wings about him; and they were full of eyes within: and they rest not day and night, saying, Holy, holy, holy, Lord God Almighty, which was and is and is to come"…"And they sing the song of Moses the servant of God, and the song of the Lamb, saying, great and marvelous are thy works, Lord God Almighty; just and true are your ways, thou King of saints…And I heard another out of the altar say, Even so, Lord God Almighty, true and righteous are thy judgments…"*
	Revelation 1:8 , *"I am Alpha and Omega, the beginning and the ending, saith the Lord, which was and is and is to come, the Almighty"…"I am Alpha and Omega, the beginning and the end, the first and the last"* (22:13)

Our Lord Yeshua/Jesus revealed Himself to Abraham, Isaac and Israel by the name God Almighty. In Genesis 49:24, it says, *"But his bow abode in strength, and the arms of his hands were made strong by the hands of the mighty God of Jacob; (from thence is the shepherd, the stone of Israel)."*

Intermittently, Abraham, Isaac, Israel, the twelve sons of Israel and the entire Israelites would call their God, the 'Almighty God' or the 'Mighty God.' In each development, they referred to the ***Salvation/Yeshua/Jesus of Israel/Nazareth***.

G. YAHWEH/JEHOVAH YESHUA/JESUS IS ABOVE ALL GODS, PRINCIPALITIES AND POWERS

<table>
<tr><th>Psalm 95: 3; 96:4-5; 97:9</th><th>John 3:31; 8:23; and Ephesians 1:21</th></tr>
<tr><td>"For the LORD is a great God, and a great King above all the earth"...
"For the LORD is great, and greatly to be praised: he is to be feared above all gods "..."For thou LORD art high above all the earth: thou art exalted above all gods"

LORD ➡ YAHWEH ➡ JEHOVAH

<table><tr><th>Part 1</th><th>Part 2</th><th>Part 3</th></tr><tr><td colspan="3">Yeshua/ Jesus/ Yahshua of Israel/Nazareth is above all gods and all principalities, powers, might, dominions and all names.</td></tr></table></td><td>"He that cometh from above is above all: he that is of the earth is earthly, and speaketh of the earth: he that cometh from heaven is above all... "And he said to
them, ye are from beneath; I am from above: ye are of this world; I am not of this world"... "Which he wrought in Christ , when he raised him from the dead, and set him at his own right hand in the heavenly
places, Far above all principality, and power, and might, and dominion, and every name that is named, not only in this world, but also in that which is to come"</td></tr>
</table>

Point 1: The LORD Yeshua/Jesus/Yahshua of Israel/Nazareth is above all gods, principalities and powers, etc.

Point 2: Yahweh Yeshua/Jesus/Yahshua of Israel/Nazareth is above all gods, principalities, powers, etc.

Point 3: Jehovah Yeshua/Jesus/Yahshua of Israel/Nazareth is above all gods, principalities, powers, etc.

H. YAHWEH/JEHOVAH YESHUA/JESUS IS THE LIVING FOUNTAIN

Jeremiah 17:13	Zechariah 12:1 0 & 13:1	Zechariah 14:8	John 19:34
"Oh LORD, the hope of Israel, all that forsake thee shall be ashamed, and they that depart from me shall be written in the earth, because they have forsaken the LORD, the fountain of living waters"	***"And I will pour upon the house of David and upon the inhabitants of Jerusalem, the spirit of grace and supplications: and they shall look upon me whom they have pierced, and they shall mourn for him, as one mourneth for his only son, and shall be in bitterness for him, as one that is in bitterness for his first born"... "And in that day there shall be a fountain opened to the house of David and to the inhabitants of Jerusalem for sin and for uncleanness"***	***"And it shall come to pass in that day, that living waters shall go out from Jerusalem; half of them toward the former sea, and half of them toward the hinder sea: in summer and in winter shall it be"***	***"But one of the soldiers with a spear pierced his side, and forthwith came there out blood and water"***

The LORD/Yahweh/Jehovah who is the fountain of living waters in Jeremiah 17:13, is also the very fountain in Zechariah 13:1 whom Yahweh/Jehovah the Father gave to be opened to the house of David (Judah) and to the inhabitants of Jerusalem because of sin and uncleanness. The living waters in Zechariah 14:8 that go out from Jerusalem are actually from the same source and this source is the LORD/Yahweh/Jehovah the Son. On the 15th Abib 30th year of the Son of God on earth in the days of Pontius Pilate, Caiaphas, Annas and Herod, He was crucified and sacrificed in Jerusalem. There in Jerusalem the 'sacrificial body' of Yahweh/Jehovah the Son who is the fountain of living waters was opened to the house of David and to the inhabitants of Jerusalem for their sins and uncleanness. In Jerusalem, a

Roman soldier pierced Yahweh/Jehovah the Son with a spear according to John 19:34. Our brother John who was in Jerusalem as an eyewitness said that when Yeshua/Jesus the fountain of living waters was pierced that blood and water came out. From that day in which our Yahweh/Jehovah the Lamb who is our fountain died, Yahweh/Jehovah the Father by His Spirit established an everlasting fountain to the house of David, to the inhabitants of Jerusalem and to the whole world for sins and for uncleanness.

When Yeshua/Jesus our Yahweh/Jehovah was wounded for our transgressions, bruised for our iniquities, chastised for our peace and His body stripped for our healing in Jerusalem, He fulfilled Jeremiah 17:13, Ezekiel 47:1-12, Zechariah 13:1 and 14:8 on the Cross of Calvary. The blood that flows from Christ's mortal wounds and bruises in conjunction with the water and blood that flows from His pierced heart have formed living waters and blood for blotting out all the sins and uncleanness of Judah, Jerusalem and the world. Just as all the Israelites passed through the red sea under Moses and Jordan under Joshua, so must all Judah, all the inhabitants of Jerusalem, and the whole world pass through the fountain of the living blood and waters of Yeshua/Jesus of Israel/Nazareth on the Cross of Calvary in Jerusalem for washing away all sins and uncleanness.

THE IMMUTABILITY OF GOD AND THE SCRIPTURES

Psalm 50:1	**Isaiah 9:6**
"The mighty God, even the LORD (Yahweh/Jehovah), hath spoken and called the earth from the rising of the sun unto the going down thereof"	***"For unto us a child is born, and unto us a son is given: and the government shall be upon His shoulder: and his name shall be called Wonderful, Counselor, The mighty God, The everlasting Father, The Prince of Peace"***

"For men verily swear by the greater: and an oath for confirmation is to them an end of all strife. Wherein God, willing more abundantly to show unto the heirs of the promise the immutability of his counsel, confirmed it by an oath: That by two immutable things, in which it was impossible for God to lie, we might have a strong consolation, who have fled for refuge to lay hold upon the hope set before us" (Hebrews 6:16-18).

The revelations of the word God in Psalm 50:1 and Isaiah 9:6 show us the eternal immutability of the immutable God and His Immutable Scriptures. Psalm 50:1 and Isaiah 9:6 are examples of the immutable seals in the Scriptures in which it is impossible for God to tell a lie. The Psalmist says that *'The Mighty God' even the LORD/Yahweh/Jehovah has spoken and called the earth from the rising of the sun unto the going down thereof*. Therefore, we say without controversy that the same 'Mighty God' (El-Gibbor) in Psalm 50:1 is also the same 'Mighty God' (El-Gibbor) in Isaiah 9:6c. This 'Mighty God' is the very 'Child born unto us' and the 'Son given unto us' whose proper name has been and will ever be called, ***'Yahweh/Jehovah the Salvation/Yeshua/Jesus of Israel.'*** Isaiah 9:6 and Proverbs 30:4 expound Psalm 2:7 about the **Sonship** of the Son of the Invisible God explicitly.

So, Charles Taze Russell and all Jehovah's Witness groups have been in dire error until date. Their blind arguments say that Yeshua/Jesus the Son of God is only called 'The Mighty God' and not 'The Almighty God' and therefore, He is not qualified to be called Yahweh/Jehovah. Since C.T. Russell was a 33rd degree Mason, with conscientious efforts he sought for a way of attacking, fighting and warring against the Saviour of Israel and the whole world. Charles C.T. Russell and all other 33rd degree Freemasons both dead and alive cannot deny the fact that they did not know from the Hebrew Bible that Yahweh/Jehovah has become the Salvation/Yeshua/Jesus of Israel/Nazareth as the Scriptures say. To the professing Jewish and Gentile Freemasons from the 1st to 33rd degrees, the Holy Spirit spoke through Apostle Paul and said,

"Because that, when they knew God, they glorified him not as God, neither were thankful; but became vain in their imaginations, and their foolish heart was darkened. Professing themselves to be wise (the enlightened ones), they became fools, And changed the glory of the incorruptible God into an image made like to corruptible man, and to birds, and four footed beasts, and creeping things. Wherefore God gave them up to uncleanness, through the lust of their hearts, to dishonor their own

bodies between themselves: who changed the truth of God into a lie, and worshipped and served the creature more than the Creator, who is blessed forever. Amen" (Emphasis mine). "For by him were all things created, that are in heaven and that are in earth, visible and invisible, whether they be thrones, or dominions, or principalities, or powers: all things were created by him and for him"

In John 1:1, C.T. Russell in the company of other high degree Freemasons changed the incorruptible Word of God who is God Himself to a 'god.' In the Bible, every translator (except C.T. Russell) assigned capital **'G'** to the Creator of the heaven and earth who the Bible calls Yeshua/Jesus of Israel and small **'g'** to the gods or vanities of the nations. Please take note of the differences in the Scriptural assertions found in John 1:1c and 2Corinthians 4:4.

John 1:1	2Corinthians 4:4
"In the beginning was the Word, and the Word was with God, and the Word was God"	***"In whom the 'god' of this world hath blinded the minds of them which believe not, lest the light of the glorious gospel of Christ, who is the image of God, should shine on them."***

When all Messianic translators referred to the Salvation/Yeshua/Jesus the Messiah of Israel in all their translations, they would assert "God" in honour of Him. However, whenever they referred to the enemy of God, angels and all men, who is Satan, they asserted small letter **'g' for** him who is called the god of this world.

When C.T. Russell in his Freemasonic translation asserted the name **'god'** (instead of God) for the Salvation/Yeshua/Jesus of Israel, who is our only

Messiah, it was a conscientious effort and pursuit of course to disdain Christ. This is because at the 28th degree of initiation in Freemasonic occult, all the initiates are taught that the ***'Salvation/Yeshua/Jesus of Israel/Nazareth'*** is the least of all the gods in the world, and as a matter of consequence, He is unworthy of any man's worship. They teach that it is an abomination to mention the name of our Lord Jesus in all Freemasonic lodges.

History also has it that the wife of C. T. Russell testified in a U.S. court that C.T. Russell was a pedophile. This confirms what is written in Romans 1:24. The Holy Ghost has given up all the Gentile and Jewish Freemasons to uncleanness. They are pedophiles, gays, ritual killers, drug peddlers, etc. Instead of worshipping and serving the blessed God and Creator—Yahweh/Jehovah who is truly Yeshua/Jesus of Israel/Nazareth, C. T. Russell and other Freemasons chose to worship and serve Lucifer who is one of the creatures of Jesus Christ of Nazareth.

MEN IN WHO IS GREAT AND GROSS DARKNESS

In Romans 1:22, the Holy Ghost says, *"Professing themselves to be wise, they became fools."* The Freemasons also call themselves the Illuminati i.e. the enlightened ones. They claim that the secrets they possess are the greatest light a man can have and attain. 85% of them are professors in various fields of human endeavours based on their crafts. They are blasphemers against the Lord Jesus. It is true that they are called the Illuminati but the questions we must ask ourselves are these, 'what nature of light is actually in them and what is the source of their light?' In the days of our Lord Jesus on earth, the Pharisees and Sadducees claimed to have light in them. They taught that men must go through them to get their own kind of light. To them our Lord Jesus said, *"But if thine eye be evil, thy whole body shall be full of darkness. If therefore the light that is in thee be darkness, how great is that darkness" (Matthew 6:23).*

Our Lord Jesus looked at the Pharisees and Sadducees who claimed to be the illuminati (enlightened ones) of their time and saw that the light in them was darkness. He interjected, 'How Great Is That Darkness.' From the st rd1 to the 33 degrees in the Freemasonic occult levels and movements, the light that is in them is 'gross darkness' and how great is that darkness, says our Lord Jesus the 'True Light' of Israel and the world. The degree of darkness that is in every Illuminati/Freemason increases grossly in an inestimable proportion as they attain higher degrees from level one to level thirty- three.

The higher the degrees they attain, the grosser the darkness becomes. Since degrees one to thirty- three expose Freemasons to the worship and service of Lucifer, it means that, the 'light' in every Mason is Lucifer and his demons. If Lucifer is the light of Freemasons, how great is the darkness in them, says our Lord Jesus the Light of Israel and the world.

Since C.T. Russell was a 33 degree Mason, oh how great is the darkness in all Jehovah's Witness members who are followers of C.T. Russell. If all the American presidents, European presidents including British prime ministers have been Freemasons that profess that they are the enlightened ones, oh how great is the darkness in them and in those nations. If all the presidents of Nigeria and Africa have been Freemasons, oh how great is the darkness in the continent of Africa. Lucifer is gross darkness and there is no iota of light in him. If all Israeli prime ministers have been Freemasons who are fighting to promote Zionism without knowing the Lamb of Zion according to Revelation 14:1-2, oh how great is the darkness in them. Please ponder over this issue, 'Can Lucifer who is gross darkness produce and give light?'

CHAPTER 10

UNDERSTANDING THE MYSTERY OF THE ALEPH-TAU

IN PSALM119:1,9,17,25,33,41,49,57,65,73,81,89,97,105,113, 121,129,137,145,153,161 and 169 IN CONNECTION WITH ISAIAH 41:4, REVELATION 2:8 AND 22:13

From the immutability of the Scriptures, we have proved that our Lord Jesus is the 'Aleph and Tau' which means the 'First and the Last.' The mystery of the 'Aleph-Tau' is a deep revelation of the Person of the Salvation/Yeshua/Jesus of Israel/Nazareth. The prophets of Israel ascribed the mystery of the 'Aleph-Tau' to Yeshua/Jesus of Israel/Nazareth only while the apostles of the Lamb confirmed it. All the apostles and disciples of Christ were students and professors in the mystery of the Salvation/Yeshua/Jesus of Israel. *"How that by revelation he made known unto me the mystery; (as I wrote afore in few words; Whereby, when ye read, ye may understand my knowledge in the mystery of Christ), Which in other ages was not made known unto the sons of men, as it is now revealed unto his holy apostles and prophets by the Spirit"* (Ephesians 3:3-5, Emphasis mine).

Please understand what the Holy Ghost made known to Apostle Paul, other holy apostles and prophets by revelation— 'The Mystery.' This 'Mystery' called the Salvation/Yeshua/Jesus of Israel/Nazareth is the bedrock of the faith of the fathers-Abraham, Isaac and Israel and ours as well. 'The Salvation/Yeshua/Jesus' of Israel = 'the Mystery' of Israel/Nazareth. He is also the 'Mystery of Africa'. When you worship the Salvation of Israel, you are worshipping the 'Mystery of Israel, Africa and the whole world. God the Father has given us the Salvation/Yeshua/Jesus of

Israel to be the 'Only Mystery' of the Israelites, Africa and the entire world. All the teachers and followers of the Salvation/Yeshua/Jesus of Israel/Nazareth are ipso facto followers of the 'Mystery' of Israel that the Holy Ghost revealed to the early church and still reveals today.

The Holy Ghost entrusted the early apostles and disciples of our Lord Jesus secular education. We have replaced the mysteries of Christ with our responsibility to cause all men to see and know the substantial reality of the fellowship of this mystery. *"And to make all men see what is the fellowship of the mystery, which from the beginning of the world hath been hid in God, who created all things by Jesus Christ"* (Ephesians 3:9). Please listen to verse 10 of Ephesians 3, from Complete Jewish Bible, *"This mystery kept hidden for ages by God the Creator of all things, is for rulers and authorities in heaven to learn through the Messianic Community (The* 1 Aleph *Church), how many sided God's wisdom is."* Our Lord Jesus is 'The Mystery' kept secret by God the Father. In the fullness of time, this Mystery became a human being by God's power. He (The Mystery) came and dwelt among men in order to teach us the mysteries of the kingdom of God.

To as many as received Him, He became their personal 'Mystery' and teacher of the mysteries of God's kingdom. Please hear 'The Mystery's voice, *"He answered and said unto them, because it is given unto thee to know the mysteries of the kingdom of heaven, but unto them it is not given"* (Matthew 13:11). All the Messianic letters of Psalm 119:1-172 are the many sided wisdom of God hidden in Yeshua/Jesus of Israel/Nazareth. This many sided wisdom of Yahweh/Jehovah the Father is not found in the Orthodox Jewish Kabala but in the 'First and Only begotten Son' of the Father.

So, originally, the Church of Yeshua/Jesus of Nazareth was set up by the Messiah through His Spirit to be a teaching institution to all powers and authorities in heavenly places. It was during the days of Paul, Peter, James, John, Andrew and other apostles that the principalities and powers in heavenly places learnt through the existence of the Church (Messianic Community), the mysteries of the Messiah. It was also in their time that the Gentile nations saw their mystic belief and practices as non-profitable adventures. When the Gentiles came to know the powers of the

'Mystery' of Israel, they offered up their charms to conflagration. *"And many that believed came, and confessed, and shewed their deeds. Many of them which had used curious arts brought their books together, and burned them before all men: and they counted the price of them, and found it fifty thousand pieces of silver"* (Acts 19:18-19). Unfortunately, it is no longer so now because of the loss of the mysteries of Christ by the present Church leaders. The reason is that in the present, 85% to 92% of our present apostles, prophets, pastors and church leaders are stark illiterate people in the mysteries of our Lord Jesus Christ in spite of their degrees in theology and church theologies and dogmas.

CHRIST IN CODED ENSIGNS

SN	SYMBOL OF ACCURACY
1	**Aleph**
Aleph stands for First. Yahweh/Jehovah is the First and this is Yeshua/Jesus of Israel. Aleph is the 'First Course' by whom all things came into existence. Aleph displays the fact that our Yeshua/Jesus will be the first Man to rise from the dead; hence, He is called the 'First Born From the Dead.' In otherwords, He is the 'First Man' born of a woman to conquer, abolish and destroy death, Satan and grave. *"And when he bringeth the first-begotten into the world, he saith, And let all the angels of God worship him"* (Hebrews 1:6). Our Lord Yeshua/Jesus is the Aleph- Son of the Father. Yahweh the Father has brought His First/**Aleph**–begotten Son into the world. His First/**Aleph** Son was the First-Man to live on earth ever before angels were created. Yeshua/Jesus is our **'Great and Ancient Aleph.'**	
2	**Beth**
Beth stands for a Tabernacle/Mishkan or House. Yahweh/Jehovah is the Tabernacle/Mishkan. In Psalm 90:1, Moses said that Yahweh/Jehovah who is Yeshua/Jesus of Israel is our dwelling place/**Beth**/Mishkan in all generations. In Hebrew 9:11, Paul, to whom the 'Mystery' was revealed among other witnesses calls Yeshua/Jesus 'The Greater and More Perfect Tabernacle/Mishkan. *"Having made known unto us the mystery of his will, according to his good pleasure which he hath purposed in himself: That in the dispensation of the fullness of times he might gather together in one all things in Christ, both which are in heaven, and which are on earth; even in him"* (Ephesians 1:9). Our heavenly Father revealed His will to the apostles in connection with the body of our Messiah Yeshua/Jesus who is the Mishkan (Tabernacle) of glory for all people. Yeshua/Jesus is the Temple/**Beth/**Mishkan in which all things in heaven and on earth would be gathered together. In the dispensation of the fullness of times, He would be the dwelling place/Mishkan/Beth for both angels and human beings and that is why He is	

called 'The Greater and More Perfect Tabernacle/Mishkan of Glory.' Yeshua/Jesus is our **'Great and Ancient Mishkan/Beth.'**	
3	**Gimmel**
Gimmel stands for Grace and Mercy. **Gimmel** stands for the Creator's overwhelming and eternal beneficence or chesed. Gimmel is a Person called Grace. The apostles and prophets knew this Person called the 'Grace' of God who is also known as the 'Grace' of Israel unto whom the disciples gathered the people. Yahweh/Jehovah Yeshua/Jesus is the Gimmel/Grace of Israel. To His throne we are invited as thus, *"Let us therefore come boldly unto the throne of grace, that we may obtain mercy, and find grace to help in time of need"* (Hebrews 4:16). Yahweh/Jehovah Yeshua/Jesus who alone is the Almighty God addresses Abraham as thus, *"After these things the word of the LORD came to Abram in a vision, saying, Fear not Abram, I am thy shield and thy exceeding great reward."* He also revealed himself to Moses as thus, *"And the LORD passed by before him, and proclaimed, The LORD, the LORD God, merciful, and gracious, long-suffering, and abundant in goodness and truth"* (Exodus 34:7). Yeshua/Jesus is our 'Great and Ancient **Gimmel.'**	
4	**Daleth**
Daleth stands for Door / Way /Gate. Yahweh/Jehovah is the Door, the Way and the Gate. In Psalm 67:1-2,the Psalmist said, *"God be merciful unto us, and bless us; and cause his face to shine upon us; That thy way (Daleth) may be known upon the earth, thy saving health among all nations..." "I am the door(Daleth)"* (John 10:9a)...*"Jesus saith unto him, I am the Way(Daleth)"* (John 14:6a)...*"But when divers were hardened, and believed not, but spake evil of that Way(Daleth) before the multitude, he departed from them, and separated the disciples, disputing in the school of one Tyrannus"*(Acts 19:9, Emphasis mine). When our Lord Yeshua/Jesus said I am the Way/**Daleth**, all His disciples knew and understood Him from Psalm 67:2, and 119:25. He is our **'Great and Ancient Daleth.'**	
5	**HEY**
Hey stands for Divine Life or Breath. Our Lord Jesus said in John 14:6c, *"I am the life..."* Then Genesis 2:7 records, *"And Yahweh/Jehovah formed man of the dust of the ground, and breathed into his nostrils the breathe (Hey) of life and man became a living soul"... "And when he hath so said this, he breathed on them, and saith unto them, Receive ye the Holy Ghost" (John 20:22).* In Genesis 2:7, the breathe/hey of Life was given to man but he lost it in the fall through sin as recorded in Genesis 3:1-9. Then in John 20:22, the 'Risen Life' gave His breath/Hey to all those men and women from the land of Israel and the Gentile nations who had believed that Yeshua/Jesus of Israel/Nazareth is both Yahweh/Jehovah and the Messiah. Through His 'Hey', all the disciples received the 'Person' of the Holy Ghost. Then at Pentecost, they all received the 'Power' of the Holy Ghost. In Genesis, 2:7 the sound of **'Hey' in man** made him a living soul.	

Then in John 20:22, the sound of ' **Hey'** was heard again which made and makes all the disciples of Christ, living spiritual men and women. *"By the word of the LORD were the heavens made; and all the host of them by the breath hey) of his mouth"* (Psalm 33:6, Emphasis mine)... *"Thus saith the Lord GOD unto these bones; behold, I will cause breath (hey) to enter into you, and ye shall* (Ezekiel 37:5). Out of the mouth of the Salvation/Yeshua/Jesus of Israel/Nazareth comes living breath (hey) that makes Israel and the Gentile nations to live. All creation is connected absolutely to the Man whose name is the 'Hey' Yeshua/Jesus of Nazareth who is Yahweh/Jehovah. He is our **'Great and Ancient Hey.'**

6	Vau or Vaw

Vaw stands for The Divine Man, Re-connector, Restorer of Judgment, Complete Redeemer, Transformer, and Reformer. **Vau** is the Messianic symbol of continuity that unites heaven and earth. After the flood of Genesis 1:2, God created man on the sixth day of the Hebrew calendar and handed the whole creation over to him. When man fell, there was a disconnection between the earth and heaven. The Creator promised to send the 'Seed' of the woman that will be the **Vau** or **Vaw** to redeem and re-connect the earth and the fallen man back to Himself. The Son of Yahweh who is called Yahwehkind or Jehovah-kind volunteered to be the **Vaw** to re-connect, redeem and reform humankind to Father Yahweh. In heaven, everlasting joy filled the hearts of the angels when the news came to them that the 'First and Only Son' of God—Yeshua/Jesus of Israel/Nazareth has volunteered to be the **Vaw** for all humanity.

Then in the sixth month of the Hebrew calendar angel Gabriel was sent from the Majesty in heaven to go and discuss about His heavenly plan with Mary. The Majesty demanded for Mary to release her womb to Him so that the **Vaw** (Re-connector, Redeemer, Restorer, and Re-former) would be born among men. Then angel Gabriel brought the good tidings to Mary who was a Hebrew woman. The Salvation /Yeshua/Jesus of Israel/Nazareth who is also called the 'Mystery' of Israel is Yahweh/Jehovah our **Vaw** on the throne of the invisible Yahweh/Jehovah the Father. *"Which only stood in meats and drinks, and divers washings, and carnal ordinances, imposed on them until the time of reformation. But Christ being come a high priest of good things to come, by a greater and more and perfect tabernacle, not made with hands, that is to say not of this building"* (Hebrews 9:10-11).

In this time of reformation, Yeshua/Jesus our **Vaw** has come to be the 'Reformer.' He formed man according to Genesis 2:7, but in Genesis 3, the Serpent or Satan deformed man through his lies. Then the Father sent His Son to come into the world and reform man with His truth. So we have *Yeshua/Jesus the former of man. *Satan the deformer of man. *Yeshua/Jesus the Christ the reformer of man. The reformation of man is only achievable through the Father's truth and not through humanity's philosophical concepts and ideologies. Yeshua/Jesus is our **'Great and Ancient Vaw.'**

7	Zayin

<table>
<tr><td colspan="2">

Zayin stands for 'The Flaming Sword', 'The Great Sword,' 'The Swore Sword' and 'The Strong Sword'... (Genesis 3:24 and Isaiah 27:1). The **Zayin** is the Messianic symbol of victory. The Salvation of Israel who is also the 'Mystery' of Israel revealed Himself to Israel the son of Isaac and said to him, 'I am your 'Flaming Sword (Zayin).' Zayin signifies spiritual struggle, as well as spiritual sustenance. In our spiritual struggle against Satan and his demons, we must know assuredly that divine victory has been promised us through Yahweh/Jehovah the Son who is our own everlasting true **Zayin**/Sword. *"Happy art thou, O Israel: who is like unto thee, O people saved by the LORD, the shield of thy help and who is the* ***Sword/ (Zayin)*** *of thy excellency! And thine enemies shall be found liars unto thee; and thou shalt tread upon their high places"* (Deuteronomy 33:29, Emphasis mine).

Here Yahweh/Jehovah is called the Sword/**Zayin** of Israel's excellency. As a student and exponent of the 'True Mystery' of Israel, Apostle Paul wrote by the Holy Ghost who is the Teacher and Revealer of this 'True Mystery,' to the church in Ephesus and other churches as well. He said, *"And take the helmet of salvation (Yeshua/Jesus) and sword* ***(Zayin)*** *of the Spirit, which is the word of God"* (Ephesians 6:17, Emphasis mine).

The 'Flaming Sword' that was placed in the Way of the Tree of Life in east of Eden is that Person whose name is 'The Word of God.' *"And his name is called the Word of God"* (Revelation 19:13b)... *"And the Word was made flesh, and dwelt among us"* (John 1:14a). The very Word of God that became flesh is also called the 'Sword of the Spirit' or '**Zayin** of the Spirit.' *"And in that day the LORD with his sore and great and strong sword shall punish leviathan the piercing serpent, even leviathan the crooked serpent; and he shall slay the dragon that is in the sea"* (Isaiah 27:1). When the Word of God became flesh and dwelt among us, it was actually the 'Sword (Zayin) of the Spirit' that the Holy Ghost revealed to humankind. So, Yeshua/Jesus of Israel/Nazareth who is Yahweh/Jehovah=The Mystery of Israel=**Zayin**/Sword of Israel/Nazareth that punishes leviathan and slays the dragon (Lucifer) that is in the sea (peoples' lives, homes, inheritances, etc). *"So he drove out the man; and he placed at the east of the garden of Eden Cherubims, and a flaming Sword/****Zayin*** *which turned every way, to keep the way of the tree of life"* (Genesis 3:24, Emphasis Mine). 'The Flaming Sword'='The Flaming Word' that was in the beginning. Yeshua/Jesus is our **'Great and Ancient Zayin.'**

</td></tr>
<tr><td>8</td><td>Chet</td></tr>
<tr><td colspan="2">

Chet stands for Life: **Chet** is a Messianic symbol of Life. In John 14:6c, Yeshua /Jesus said, *"I am the Life."* When He said to them, *I am the Life*, they understood that He said I am the **Chet**. He is the **Chet** (Life) whose breath made man a living soul. He is the Life/**Chet** in all creation. He is the indestructible Life/**Chet**. He is our sign of 'Transcendence and of Divine Grace.' Through Yeshua/Jesus Messiah we can transcend the limitations of physical existence i.e. go beyond all the usual limits of something. Nothing limits the Almighty Yahweh/Jehovah Yeshua/Jesus of Israel/Nazareth who alone is the 'Eternal and Ancient **Chet**.' He takes us beyond the realms of limitations just as He took the saints out of the limitations of sin and death. Yeshua/Jesus is our **'Great and Ancient Chet'**

</td></tr>
</table>

9	Teth
Teth is an epitome of 'Goodness and Humility.' **Teth** means the 'Good One' or the 'Good Word of God.' *"And have tasted the good word of God"* (Hebrews 6:5a). It also means to sweep out the 'Evil One' by the 'Good One' through judgment. *"Shall not the judge of the earth do right"* (Genesis 18:25c). Psalm 136:1-end, expresses the goodness of Yahweh/Jehovah our God to Israel. The Salvation/Yeshua/Jesus of Nazareth is a total epitome of 'Goodness and Humility.' *"And how God anointed Jesus of Nazareth with the Holy Ghost and power: who went about doing good, and healing all that were oppressed of the devil; for God was with him"*(Acts 10:38). He is the 'Good One/**Teth**' that goes about doing good and healing all that are oppressed of the devil. His goodness and humility enriched and still enriches humanity. Through the goodness of the 'Good One', He sweeps out the devil which oppresses us by His judgment. He is the very one that the Psalmist wrote about His goodness to Israel in Psalm 136. In this world of evil, Yeshua/Jesus of Israel is our Good One/ **Teth**. "*Surely, his goodness **(Teth)** will follow me, all the days of my life and I will dwell in the house (Beth) of the LORD/Yahweh/Jehovah forever"* (Psalm 23:6). Yeshua/Jesus is our **'Great and Ancient Teth.**	
10	**Yodh**
Yodh means hands. It signifies the Creator's hands in all His creation. *"Thy hands (Yodh) have made me and fashioned me: give me understanding, that I may learn thy commandments*" (Psalm 119:73, Emphasis Mine). King David acknowledged the hands that made him. By this statement, he implies that he did not evolve. He confessed that he was created. No true child of Israel believes in evolution theory because the Hebrews and their Hebrew Bible teach that the creation came into being by the Yodh/hands of Yahweh/Jehovah of Israel who is Yeshua/Jesus of Israel. In the creation of angels, the **Yod**h/hands of the God of Israel formed and made them all. *"Thou wast perfect in thy ways from the day thou was created, till iniquity was found in thee"* (Ezekiel 28:15). Even the Hebrew Bible testifies that Lucifer did not evolve but was created just like every other creature. *"The right hand (Yodh) of the LORD doeth valiantly. The right hand/Yodh of the LORD is exalted"* (Psalm 118:15b). *"Both riches and honour come of thee, and thou reignest over all, and in thine hand **(Yodh)** is power and might; and in thy hand it is to make great, and to give strength to all" (1 Chronicles 29:12). "Humble yourself therefore under the mighty hand/**Yodh** of God, that he may exalt you in due time" (1Peter* 5:6). The hand/**Yodh** of Yahweh/Jehovah who is Yeshua/Jesus of Israel/Nazareth has formed all creation. The signature of His hands is in every visible and invisible creation. Yeshua/Jesus is our **'Great and Anicent Yodh.**	
11	**Kaph**

Kaph is a symbol of 'Crowning Accomplishments.'
Kaph relates to the principles of the four crowns and these four crowns are the *'Priesthood,'* the *'Kingship,'* the *'Torah or the Word'* of God and a *'Good Name.'* Consequently, only Jesus perfectly fits into these four crowns.
**Yeshua/Jesus is our great High Priest from Judah by the sworn oath of Yahweh/Jehovah the Father after the order of Melchizedek. *"For it is evident that our Lord sprang out of Judah; of which tribe Moses spake nothing concerning priesthood"* (Hebrews 7:14).

The sacrifices of the Levitical priests only brought men to the ark of the Old Testament in Jerusalem but the sacrifice that Yeshua/Jesus our 'Great High Priest' from Judah made in Jerusalem in the days of His flesh, brings all men and women to the temple of God in heaven where we see the ark of the 'New Testament.' His priesthood that was rooted in obedience to His death on the Cross crowns us to become His Father's priests in order to serve Him.

**Yeshua/Jesus of Israel/Nazareth is our only true King. *"Yet have I set my king upon my holy hill of Zion"* (Psalm 2:6). The Salvation/Yeshua/Jesus of Israel/ Nazareth is both the Father's King as well as Israel's King. The Father Yahweh's Son was the Person who changed Jacob's name to Israel. Yeshua/Jesus who is the 'Mystery' of Israel is also the King of Israel. Both our Father Yahweh and Israel the son of Isaac share a 'Common King' together and this very King is Yeshua/Jesus. In other words, Yeshua/Jesus is the Commonwealth of the Father Yahweh/Jehovah and Israel. He is our heavenly Father's King sent to the earth that the Bible calls the King of Glory.

In Zechariah9:9, He is called the King of Zion and Jerusalem. According to Matthew 5:35, Yeshua/Jesus of Israel/Nazareth is the sole heir of Jerusalem. In the book of Revelation 1:6, this great King that unites heaven and earth makes all the believers in Him kings and priests unto His blessed Father and ours. He offered up His priestly and kingly body and blood to be the 'Last Sacrifice' to redeem us from Satan and sin.
**Yeshua/Jesus is the Living Torah/Word of God. *"In the beginning was the Word (Torah) and the Word (Torah) was with God and the Word (Torah) was God"* (John 1:1). The Living Word/Torah that became a human being for the sake of redemption existed in everlasting and in ancient times. Yahweh/Jehovah the Son even Yeshua of Israel is the 'Ancient One. Nevertheless, He is not old. If we give heed to the 'Ancient Word' of God, He will crown us with His ancient crown in glory. In Matthew 17:5, Yahweh/Jehovah the Father calls us to hear His Ancient Word/Torah who has become His Son in human flesh.
**Yahweh/Jehovah is the only 'Good Name.' When we receive Yeshua/Jesus of Nazareth, our names and persons become good in the sight of all of heaven and our Father. Yahweh/Jehovah, which is a communicable good name among angels and his creation, is a great crown. "A good name is better than precious ointment" (Ecclesiastes 7:1a). .. *"Being made so much better that the angels, as he hath by inheritance obtained a more excellent*

name than they" (Hebrews 1:4). Our primary objective must be a pursuit towards a good name in Yahweh/Jehovah Yeshua/Jesus of Israel. Only the Father, the Son and the Holy Ghost has a good name. Yahweh/Jehovah is a communicable and not an ineffable name. When we receive Yeshua/Jesus of Israel/Nazareth, we become heirs and joint heirs with His Priesthood, Kingship, the Living Word and the Good Name. Yeshua/Jesus is indeed our **'Great and Ancient Kaph.'**	
12	**Lamed**

Lamed is a symbol of Wisdom and purpose. It symbolizes the King of kings and the Supreme Ruler. Yeshua/Jesus is the 'Ancient and Absolute Wisdom and Purpose that rules supremely.' *"But unto them which are called, both Jews and Greeks, Christ the power of God, and the wisdom of God"* (1Corinthians 1:24).
The early apostles taught the Gentiles to whom they were sent the mysteries of the Messiah/Christ who is Yeshua/Jesus of Nazareth the Supreme King. Therefore, Yeshua/Jesus who is Yahweh-kind or Jehovah-kind is the **Lamed**/Wisdom of the Father that ruled over Abraham, Isaac, Israel. He is the 'Supreme Ruler' over all men and angels. He is the express Wisdom/**Lamed** of God dwelling in us.
This **Lamed** existed in everlasting and in ancient times. He is above all mysticism and all wisdom of the world. King Solomon who asked for **Lamed**/Wisdom in order for him to be a great and wise king, spoke of the Person of **Lamed** in that followed and blessed Solomon is Yeshua/Jesus of Israel the ancient Wisdom of their fathers.
"And when the Sabbath day was come, he began to teach in the synagogue: and many hearing him were astonished, saying, From whence hath this man these things? and what wisdom(Lamed) is this which is given unto him, that even such mighty works are wrought by his hands/yodh"(Mark 6:2)... "In whom are hid all the treasures of wisdom and knowledge" (Colossians 2:3). Knowledge equals purpose. Our Father Yahweh has reserved all the treasures of wisdom and purpose in Yeshua/Jesus His Son and not in the kabala of Freemasons. Therefore, the kabala or secrets of Freemasons/Illuminati are deceitful, empty and false wisdom.
If you know the truth that, He is our 'Ancient Lamed' you will be set free from false wisdom and mysticism. The question that the Jews asked in Mark 6:2 was answered in Colossians 2:3. In proverbs 8:12, Yeshua/Jesus of Israel is the metaphorical Lamed that dwells with prudence. "I wisdom (Lamed) dwell with prudence, and find knowledge (purpose) of witty inventions" (Proverbs 8:12, Emphasis Mine)... "My mouth shall speak of wisdom; and the meditation of my

heart shall be of understanding" (Psalm 49:3).
The true leaders in Israel such as David, Asaph, Korah, Solomon, etc. were students and teachers of the Lamed of Israel. The 'Great Lamed' who is the Salvation/Yeshua/Jesus of Israel/Nazareth appeared to those fathers just as He appeared to Abraham, Isaac and Israel and taught them the 'Ancient Wisdom' of the 'The Great White Throne.' To David, Lamed the King of kings taught the wisdom of warfare against the kings just as He taught Abraham the wisdom of warfare against Amraphael and his allies.

Proverbs 8:12, shows that Yeshua/Jesus, who is the living Lamed, is the inventor/Creator of all angels and human beings. He invented redemption and reconciliation through His death on the Cross of Calvary. He also through His death invented the weapon (His blood) that destroys hell, death and Satan. His own blood is destructive to his enemies.
He is the inventor of the heavens, the earth, the mountains, the sea, the air, the trees etc. "Wisdom is the principle thing; therefore get wisdom: and with all thy getting get understanding" (Proverbs 4:7). Yeshua/Jesus of Israel/Nazareth who is our 'Supreme Lamed' is the principle thing in the lives of the men and women of Israel and others. He is our 'Preeminent One' and 'Holy One.' This implies that He is the 'Principal Person' among angels and men in the affairs of heaven and earth.
The ancient fathers of Israel taught their children that in all their pursuits in life, they should first know the ruling Wisdom/Lamed of Israel. They also educated them in all their pursuits to get to know Understanding. Yeshua/Jesus who is the 'Sole Mystery' of Israel is also the Wisdom and Understanding to all the Israelites and others who would seek Him wholeheartedly in their schools at kindergarten, primary and tertiary levels.
"But where shall wisdom/Lamed be found? And where is the place of understanding? Man knoweth not the price thereof; neither is it found in the land of the living. The depth saith, It is not in me: and the sea saith, It is not with me. Whence then cometh wisdom? And where is the place of understanding? "Destruction and death say, We have heard the fame thereof with our ears. God understandeth the way thereof, and he knoweth the place thereof" (Job 28:12-14, 20, 22 & 23, Emphasis Mine). The answer to the first question in Job 28:12 is given in John 1:1c, "And the Word/Lamed was with God." Then the second answer to the question in Job 28:20 which says, Whence cometh wisdom...is

<table>
<tr><td colspan="2">given in John 16:28, "I came forth from the Father, and I am come into the world: again I leave the world and go to the Father.
Long before Yeshua/Jesus of Israel/Nazareth, our 'Wisdom/Lamed' became a human being, destruction and death heard His fame. As He became a legitimate human being for our redemption, both of them saw His fame through His miracles, His death on the Cross-and His resurrection from the dead. Through His famous death on the Cross and resurrection from the dead, Yeshua/Jesus of Israel/Nazareth destroyed Satan and abolished death forever.
"Forasmuch then as the children are partakers of flesh and blood, he also himself likewise took part of the same; that through death he might destroy him that had the power of death, that is, the devil" (Hebrews 2:14)... "But is now made manifest by the appearing of our Saviour Jesus Christ, who hath abolished death, and hath brought life and immortality to light through the gospel" (2Timothy 1:10). Yeshua/Jesus is our 'Great and Ancient Lamed.'</td></tr>
<tr><td>13</td><td>Mem</td></tr>
<tr><td colspan="2">Mem stands for the 'Revealed One' or 'The Revealed Messiah.' Yeshua/Jesus of Israel/Nazareth is the revealed evidence of the sovereignty of God over His creation. Mem symbolizes the 'Sovereignty of the Messiah of Israel/Nazareth' or the 'Sovereign One.' To His eternal Sovereignty, John the Baptist testifies, "John answered, saying unto them all, I indeed baptize you with water; but one mightier than I cometh, the latchet of whose shoes I am not worthy to unloose: he shall baptize you with the Holy Ghost and fire" (Luke 3:16). "Verily I say unto you, Among them that are born of women there hath not risen a greater than John the Baptist" (Matthew 11:11a). John the Baptist who was mighty and great said that someone is coming who is mightier than he is even Yeshua/Jesus. "Before the LORD: for he cometh to judge the earth: he shall judge the world with righteousness and the people with his truth" (Psalm 96:13).
In the creation of the earth, Yeshua/Jesus of Israel who is our 'Sovereign Messiah' gave man sovereignty over the works of His hands/yodh. "Thou madest him to have dominion over the works of thine hands; thou has put all things under his feet' (Psalm 8:6). "And they feared exceedingly, and said one to another, What manner of man is this, that even the wind and the sea obey him?" (Mark 4:41). The question here is, 'What manner of man is this that the wind and the sea obey him?'
The absolute answer to this question is, Yeshua/Jesus of Nazareth is Yahweh/Jehovah our Mem who became a human being in order to save us from</td></tr>
</table>

all natural disasters and from Satan. "O LORD God of hosts, who is a strong LORD like unto thee? or to thy faithfulness round about thee? Thou rulest the raging of the sea; when the waves thereof arise, thou stillest them" (Psalm 89:8-9)... "And he was in the hinder part of the ship, asleep on a pillow: and they awake him, and say unto him, Master, carest thou not that we perish? And he arose, and rebuked the wind, and said unto the sea, Peace, be still. And the wind ceased, and there was a great calm" (Mark 4:38-39). Please meditate (selah) on the underlined words stillest and still in Psalm 89:9 and Mark 4:39 respectively.

In the Old Testament, only Yahweh/Jehovah has authority to rebuke evil and in the New Testament we see Yeshua/Jesus rebuking the wind and at the same time speaking to the sea. Does this not teach us that Yeshua/Jesus of Nazareth is Yahweh/Jehovah in human form? "That saith to the deep, Be dry, and I will dry up thy rivers" (Isaiah 44:27)... "I say to the deep sea, 'Dry up! I will make your streams run dry" (Complete Jewish Bible)... "It is I who says to the depths of the sea, 'be dried up!' I will make your rivers dry" (New American Standard Version)... "With a word of command I dry up the ocean" (Good News Translation).

In the book of Mark 4:39, we see our Lord Yeshua/Jesus silencing and calming the raging of the sea with His word of command. "Which stillest the noise of the seas, the noise of their waves, and the tumult of the people" (Psalm 65:7)... "Which rebuked the red sea also, and it was dried up: so he led them through the depths, as through the wilderness" (Psalm 106:9). He is the 'Revealed Mystery' of heaven that reveals the mysteries of the kingdom of heaven to men and saves us from mysticisms and mythologies of demons. He reveals to us the concealed rule of heaven over all things.

Humanity must submit in faith of Him alone because Yeshua/Jesus is the 'Ancient Mem.' Mem is the sign of the Messiah and this was revealed to Daniel by angel Gabriel according to Daniel 9:24-25. To Yahweh/Jehovah Yeshua/Jesus, our Mem will all people, nations, languages, and tongues serve and worship according to Daniel 7:9 & 13. Yeshua/Jesus is our 'Great and Ancient Mem.'

14	**Nun**
Nun symbolizes the 'Great Light or Brightness' for the people in darkness. "The people that walked in darkness have seen a great light: they that dwell in the land of the shadow of death, upon them hath the light shined" (Isaiah 9:2). Nun also stands for the everlasting faithfulness of the Messiah. It shows the nature of His Word to us in the person of the Light and Lamp. Yeshua/Jesus of Israel is the	

eternal Lamp. "Then spake Jesus again unto them saying, I am the light of the world: he that followeth me shall not walk in darkness but shall have the light of life" (John 8:12). In Revelation 1:5, our Lord is called the faithful witness. In Revelation 19:11, His name is faithful and true. "And the light/Nun shineth in darkness and the darkness comprehended it not. That was the true Light/Nun which lighteth every man that cometh into the world" (John 1:5, 9, Emphasis Mine). In a deeper sense of meaning, Nun represents the 'emergence of the soul or a being'.

In creation man became an emerged soul or being through the breath of our Lord Jesus Christ but this soul failed God through sin. Then in the redemption, the Torah/the Word of God emerged to become the 'Living Legitimate Being' through legitimate physical birth, so that He would be the true Light/Nun of the world. Those who receive Him and say, 'Lord Yeshua/Jesus you are the Nun of Israel' are called the sons and daughters of the 'Great Light' of Israel while those who reject Him are called the children of 'Gross Darkness' no matter how enlightened they claim to be.

Yeshua/ Jesus of Israel/Nazareth is the emerged 'Divine Being' whose precious and sinless soul was made an offering and a ransom for our sins and death. "Yet it pleased the LORD to bruise him; he hath put him to grief: when thou shalt make his soul an offering for sin, he shall see his seed, he shall prolong his days, and the pleasure of the LORD shall prosper in his hands" (Isaiah 53:10, Emphasis Mine). He is the emerged Nun in human form whose soul, hell could not hold. He being our Nun is the available grace of God to us. If you receive this eternal Nun and release your own soul to Him, He will keep your soul from the hunt of hell and death. In Acts 26:13, Yeshua/Jesus of Israel who is the Nun above the brightness of the sun appeared to save Paul from the gross darkness of his fathers' traditions.

Nevertheless, He is not the molded images you see in Roman Catholic, or the pictures of Orthodox and Pentecostal churches. He is 'The Great White Light' from 'The Great white Throne' that enlightens all men in all generations. He revealed and still reveals Himself in the person of the 'Great White Light' of the people. In Psalm 27:1a, king David who knew Yeshua/Jesus of Israel acclaimed Him to be his Light/Nun that delivered him from all his fears. In Isaiah 60:1, the prophet Isaiah through the Holy Ghost called on the people of Israel to arise and shine because their Nun, which is Yeshua/Jesus of Israel/Nazareth has come. Anybody in Israel who received Yeshua/Jesus our true Nun shone brightly but all that refused Him wallowed in gross darkness. In this modern era, the situation is

<table>
<tr><td colspan="2">also applicable to all who refuse Him. He is the 'Ancient Nun' of Abraham, Isaac and Israel that made the sun, the moon and the stars. "Giving thanks unto the Father, which hath made us meet to be partakers of the inheritance of the saints in light/Nun" (Colossians 1:12). All the true saints in Christ Yeshua/Jesus dwell in Nun. Yeshua/Jesus is our 'Great and Ancient Nun'</td></tr>
<tr><td>15</td><td>Samech</td></tr>
<tr><td colspan="2"><u>Samech</u> symbolizes Divine Support, Trust, Dependence and Protection. "The eternal God is thy refuge, and underneath are the everlasting arms: and he shall trust out the enemy from before thee; and shall say, destroy them" (Deuteronomy 33:27). <u>Samech</u> is also associated with memory. Yeshua/Jesus of Israel/Nazareth is our <u>Samech</u> who divinely supports us. He is trustworthy, dependable and supportive. All sinners and saints are under Christ's divine support and protection. "While I was in the world, I guarded (protected) them by the power of your name, which you have given to me; yes I kept watch over them" (John 17:12a, Complete Jewish Bible). As I said, it is also associated with memory. In terms of the memory, our Saviour who is our <u>Samech</u> helps our dull memories and activates them to comprehend the mysteries of the kingdom of heaven.
The Holy Ghost wants us to exact the power of our memory or mind in reading and understanding the things about our Messiah Jesus. Our Lord Jesus has trusted us to the care of the Holy Ghost who teaches and opens our memories for active comprehension of the ancient realities of heaven as expressed in the Bible only. In secular education, educationists only impart knowledge, nevertheless, they do not have the power to activate or enlarge the memory of students. However, in the divine education that offers knowledge on the mysteries of the Messiah, the Holy Ghost imparts unto us God's ancient words and knowledge as He enlarges and activates our memory. Part of the works of the Holy Spirit is that He also helps to enlarge, protect and support our memories for active comprehension. "And he holds everything together" (Colossians 1:17b). Here apostle Paul who was a degree holder in the mysteries of 'The Mystery' of Israel shows us that Yeshua/Jesus of Israel is the true Samech who holds all things together— all the angels, human beings and the cosmos. Yeshua/Jesus is the 'Great and Ancient Samech.'</td></tr>
<tr><td>16</td><td>Ayin</td></tr>
<tr><td colspan="2">Ayin means eyes, source, centre or wellspring. Yeshua/Jesus of Israel/Nazareth is the only</td></tr>
</table>

true source, centre and wellspring of all things in heaven and earth. Ayin is a symbol of perception and insight both of the physical and spiritual eye. Matthew 6:18 speaks of the eyes that see in the secret. "For the eyes of the LORD run to and fro throughout the whole earth, to show himself strong in the behalf of them whose heart is perfect towards him"(2chronicles 16:9a). While the Gentile nations taught and believed in the eye of the Horus, the true fathers in Israel taught their people about the eyes of Yahweh/Jehovah that run to and fro throughout the whole earth. Our Lord Jesus who is the true Ayin sees the whole earth and every activity therein. It takes our Ayin negligible seconds to run back and forth the whole earth.

Before Him who is our Ayin, hell and death are stark naked. "Neither is there any creature that is not manifest in his sight: but all are naked and opened unto the eyes of him with whom we have to do" (Hebrews 4:13). Before Yeshua/Jesus who is Jehovah, the Egyptian Eye of the Horus (Sun) is gross darkness. Whom do you serve and worship— the 'Ancient Ayin' who is the Messiah Yeshua/Jesus or the Egyptian Eye of the Horus? Only Jesus Christ is our eternal perception and insight. Matthew 6:22a says, "For the light of the body is the eye (ayin): If therefore thine eye (ayin) be single, thy whole body shall be full of light." The eye/ayin is the light of the body.

If we make Yeshua/Jesus of Nazareth our Ayin, we shall have great light within us but if we make the eye/ayin of the Horus (sun) our eye, we shall have gross darkness within and as a matter of consequence, roam about in great darkness. Yeshua/Jesus wants to become our Ayin so that we can see into the realm of our Father's kingdom. He being the Ayin is the microcosm of the universe. He is the wellspring of all eyes both in heaven and on earth. Yeshua/Jesus of Israel is the true centre of gravity according to Isaiah 40:22. The Egyptian Horus (Sun) which claims to be the eye or centre of gravity, source or wellspring is false. All the heavenly luminaries are under the eyes of Yeshua/Jesus of Israel that pace back and forth within split seconds. Yeshua/Jesus is the **'Great and Ancient Ayin.'**

17	**Pey**

Pey means Mouth. It represents both speech and silence. In addition, it is closely linked to healing. Our Lord Jesus is the living Mouth/Pey that speaks for humanity. The Lord Yeshua/Jesus who is the living Pey spoke all things into existence. Whenever Yeshua/Jesus of Israel opens His mouth, speech, power, life, etc. flow out to His creation. He is the unlimited utterance of Israel.

The Holy Ghost is inviting us to feed from the proceedings of the mouth/Pey of our Lord Jesus Christ. "But he answered and said, It is written, Man shall not live by bread alone but by every word that proceedeth out of the mouth/Pey of God" (Matthew 4:4). And out of his mouth (pey) went (goes) out a sharp double- edged sword (Revelation 1:16b). The Lord Yeshua/Jesus is our 'Ancient Pey who releases a sharp two edged sword that destroys His enemies and all physical weapons of war.

If we live by every word that flows out of our 'Living Pey,' we will not fear any weapons. In the book of Daniel 7:20, we see a mouth (pey) that spoke overwhelming things against God and His saints. Apparently, there are mouths that are speaking great things against us and our God and we can only confront and deal with them by knowing that Yeshua/Jesus is our sovereign Pey. The mouth/pey is closely linked with the art of healing. Sound Pey brings sound healing and only Jesus is our sound Pey. "For the priest's lips should keep knowledge, and they should seek the law at his mouth/pey: for he is the messenger of the LORD of hosts" (Malachi 2:7, Emphasis Mine).

The mouth of every priest whether a Satanist or Messianic, is more powerful than the mouth of an ordinary person. King Ballack sought for a curse from the mouth of Balaam who was a priest or more correctly, a soothsayer because they believed that whatever his mouth spoke had the power to frustrate the Israelites on their journey into the promised land.

Our Lord Jesus is our 'Eternal and Great High Priest and Pey' from whom we can have true reality. In Luke 21:15, Yeshua/Jesus who is our only true Pey promised to give us a mouth/pey and wisdom which all our adversaries shall not be able to gainsay or resist. Psalm 8:2 speaks of the pey of babies and suckling. Indeed, the Holy Ghost really wants to silence the enemy and the avenger through the pey of God's children; however, this is only possible when His children learn to live by the word proceeding from our true **Pey**.

Finally, the ultimate purpose of creation is for human kind to learn to sing the praises of the Almighty God and study the Bible. This is the highest purpose of life. Moses spent the rest of his life singing the praises of the Almighty Yeshua/Jesus of Israel, studying and teaching His fiery words. King David spent his years in singing the praises of the Almighty King and God of Israel, studying and teaching His word. Through this means, they all did great exploits in all their generations. Purity, holiness, healing, power and uncompromising love flow from our singing the praises of Yeshua/Jesus/ of Israel/Nazareth, for His accomplished works of redemption on the cross of Calvary, hearing and studying His words according to Matthew 17:5 and teaching the mysteries that proceed from His mouth.

"Let the words of Christ dwell in you richly in all wisdom; teaching and admonishing one another in psalms, and hymns and spiritual songs, singing with grace in your hearts to the Lord" (Colossians 3:10). Yeshua/Jesus is the **'Great and Ancient Pey.**

18	**Tzaddik**

Tzaddik stands for 'The Righteous or the Just and the Humble One.' It stands for Righteousness and Justice. "Which of the prophets have not your fathers persecuted? and they have slain them which shewed before of the Just One: of whom ye have been now the betrayers and murderers" (Acts 7:52). Here we see Stephen rebuking the Jews for killing the Just or the Righteous One/Tzaddik who is equally the Holy One of God and of Israel. Psalm 119:137 actually begins this way, "Righteous are thou, oh LORD/Yahweh/Jehovah and upright are thy judgments…" (Emphasis Mine). In John 17:25, Yeshua/Jesus, who is the visible Tzaddik of Israel, addressed the invisible Father as thus, "Oh righteous (Tzaddik) Father." Therefore, Yeshua/Jesus of Nazareth is the visible, literal Tzaddik/Just One of the invisible Tzaddik Abba (Righteous Father) in heaven just as He is the visible Yahweh/Jehovah of the invisible Yahweh/Jehovah in heaven. Yeshua/Jesus of Israel/Nazareth is the very Person addressed by Moses in Deuteronomy 32:4 as the 'Upright and Righteous.' It is only in Yeshua/Jesus that we have true righteousness. He is our

'Supreme Tzaddik' that makes us righteous through His blood and resurrection. He is the righteous and the humble Lamb sacrificed for us. Only those people who have been made righteous by His Son's blood, does our Father accept into His kingdom. "Righteousness (Tzaddik) exalts a nation: but sin (Satan) is a reproach to any people" (Proverbs 14:34, Emphasis Mine). It means that the Tzaddik/Righteous/Just/Humble One exalts a nation as well as an individual.' Yeshua/Jesus of Israel/Nazareth is the 'Righteousness/Tzaddik that exalted Abraham, Isaac, Israel, Judah, Moses, David, Solomon and others at individual levels. Through the great leaders of Israel who were followers of the Tzaddik of Israel, He exalted Israel as a nation. Through the apostles and prophets who knew and followed Him when He came in human flesh to be 'The Righteous Reformer,' the early church was exalted above the world in all things. He is the Tzaddik/Righteous One that exalted all the apostles and prophets we read about in the New Testament. Satan is the 'Sin' that stood at the door of Cain's life which brought upon him perpetual reproach according to Genesis 4:7. When men like Rehoboam, Manasseh, Ahab, Coniah, etc. departed from Yeshua/Jesus of Israel who is the 'Righteousness/Tzaddik' of their fathers, and turned to Satan who is metaphorically 'Sin' in Proverbs 14:34b, untold reproaches came upon Israel. Satan is synonymous with reproach. Where Satan abounds, sin abounds as well as reproaches. If you embrace Yeshua/Jesus of Nazareth, He will become your glorified Tzaddik. He will cleanse you from all reproaches of life. Yeshua/Jesus is our **'Great and Ancient Tzaddik.'**	
19	**Quf**
Quf stands for 'Holiness.' From Quf we have Qodesh or Kadosh. It is for both human beings and the Divine One. In John 17:11 we see the blessed Son of the blessed Father calling our Father 'holy' as thus, "And now I am no more in the world, but these are in the world, and I come to thee. Holy Father, keep through thine own name those whom thou hast given me, that they may be one, as we are one." 'Holy Father' here means in Hebrews 'Qodesh Abba'. In Acts 4:27, it says, "For a truth against thy holy (qodesh/kadosh) son, whom thou hast anointed"… "And the four beasts had each one of them six wings about him; and they were full of eyes within: and they rest not day and night, saying, Holy, holy, holy, Lord God Almighty, which was, and is, and is to come" (Revelation 4:8). Our Master Yeshua/Jesus is the one who was dead in Jerusalem, and is now alive through physical resurrection and is coming again with the Father's glory and in tremendous power. The Spirit of the Father and His Son is holiness/**Quf.** His Holy Spirit is called 'Ruach Hakodesh' in Hebrew language. Quf helps us to depart from sin and all abominations. "In that day shall there be upon the bells of the horses, HOLINEES UNTO THE LORD; and the pots in the LORD's house shall be like the bowls before the altar" (Zechariah 14:20). The mystery of Quf is the Person of Yeshua/Jesus who is both the Holy One of God and Israel. He is the Commonwealth of God in heaven and all the Messianic Hebrews and Gentiles. We attain qodesh or holiness through the precious blood of the Lamb of God slaughtered in Jerusalem for us. Please understand that 'Quf or Kadosh' is a Person and not just	

<table>
<tr><td colspan="2">a symbol and that this Person has sent His Spirit (Ruach) to us for Him to guide us into the path of 'Ancient Holiness.' If you acknowledge Yeshua/Jesus who has become our indispensable Quf/Holiness, He will send His Holy Spirit upon you. His Person, His words, His blood and His Spirit are holy. Today, the heaven and earth are not looking for men of God but for holy men of God who are led by the Holy Spirit. The creation is looking for them simply because they have yielded their souls to Yeshua/Jesus the Holy One of Israel. Yeshua/Jesus is our 'Great and Ancient Quf.'</td></tr>
<tr><td>20</td><td>Resh/Rosh</td></tr>
<tr><td colspan="2">Resh/Rosh stands for 'The Head, Chieftain or Supreme One'. "Thine, O LORD, is the greatness, and the power, and the glory, and the victory, and the majesty: for all that is in the heaven and in the earth is thine; thine is the kingdom, O LORD, and thou art exalted as head/Rosh above all" (Chronicles 29:11, Emphasis Mine). All the prophets in the Old Testament knew that our Lord Yeshua/Jesus is the exalted Head/Rosh as they all wrote about Him. Rosh means the 'Preeminent One' from heaven. He is both the Head of all angels, human beings and the entire creation. "And He is the head/Rosh of the body, the church: who is the beginning, the firstborn from the dead that in all things he might have the preeminence"... "And ye are complete in him, which is the head/Rosh of all principality and power" (Colossians 2:10). He is the exalted Rosh above heaven and earth. "And not holding the Head/Rosh, from which all the body by joints and bands having nourishment ministered, and knit together, increaseth with the increase of God" (Colossians 1:29). Here apostle Paul refers to people who are not holding to Yeshua/Jesus who is the true Head/Rosh. The Rosh of Psalm 119:153 is a Person and not just a symbol. "And hath put all things under his feet and gave him to be the head/Rosh over all things to the church" (Ephesians 1:22). Our dear heavenly Father has given our Lord Yeshua/Jesus to us to be the 'Everlasting Rosh' to His churches in all things. In Revelation 1:14 John saw the splendor of Yeshua/Jesus our Rosh/Head. He said that the head and hairs of our Head/Rosh were (and are still) as white like wool and as white as snow. Through Yeshua/Jesus our Resh, we are delivered from the degradations of life and catapulted into His greatness. In Acts 10:38 and Isaiah 61:1, we see the 'Anointed' Yahweh/Jehovah the Son, by the Spirit of Yahweh the Father. Yahweh the Father anointed His own 'Kind' and gave Him to the world to be the Head/Resh of all human beings and Great High Priest amongst us by the seal of the Holy Spirit.
The oil flowing from the head of this 'Great High Priest' after the order of</td></tr>
</table>

Melchizedek is far much greater and glorious than the oil that flowed from the head and beard of Aaron according to Psalm 132:2. If we submit our own head (rosh) to the 'Ancient Head/Rosh of the Lord Jesus, His own living, holy and pure oil will overflow and ever flow through us. He anoints us by His Spirit to become heads under him. In Deuteronomy 28:13, it says that the LORD shall make you the head (rosh) and not the tail. It is only when Yeshua/Jesus of Israel/Nazareth becomes our true Rosh/Head that our heads will be lifted up. He deserves our worship. Yeshua/Jesus is our **'Great and Ancient Rosh.'** (Emphasis Mine).	
21	**Shin or Schin**
Shin or Schin stands for 'Divine Peace, Power and Majesty. Yeshua/Jesus of Israel our Messiah commanded the Israelites to attach this ensign called 'Schin on their doorposts. In the past, all the Jewish doorposts had the bill of Schin strongly attached to them because it is one of the awesome manifestations of the Salvation/Yeshua/Jesus of Israel to them in all their dwellings. In these last days, it will be good for us who have come to trust in Yeshua/Jesus of Israel to have the bill of Schin strongly attached to our doorposts. It is a sign of El- Shaddai, which was revealed to Abraham in Genesis 17:1 when Yeshua/Jesus our Lord visited Abraham and Sarah. If we want to exude divine peace, power and majesty, we must come into uncompromising terms with the truth that Yeshua/Jesus of Israel is the Schin. The pictorial symbol of Schin signifies the inseparable bond between Yahweh the Father, Yahweh the Son and Yahweh the Holy Ghost on the 'Great White Throne' of heaven because the Father, His Son and His Holy Spirit share one throne. Please receive Yeshua/Jesus to be your personal and family Schin. The Divine Peace, Power and Majesty of Yeshua/Jesus our Schin will keep you throughout your days on earth. Halleluiah! Yeshua/Jesus is our **'Great and Ancient Schin.'**	
22	**TAU**
Tau stands for the ensign. "And in that day there shall be a root of Jesse, which shall stand as an ensign of the people; to it shall the Gentiles seek: and his rest shall be glorious" (Isaiah 11:10)… "And one of the elders saith unto me, Weep not: behold, the Lion of the tribe of Judah, the root of David, hath prevailed to open the book and to loose the seals thereof" (Revelation5:5)… "I am the root and offspring of David, and the bright and morning star" (Revelation 22:16). Tau is a symbol or ensign of the 'Last Sacrifice.' The book of Isaiah 11:10 says, "And in that day there shall be a root of Jesse, which shall stand for an ensign of the people; to it shall the Gentiles seek: and His rest shall be glorious." The Salvation/Yeshua/Jesus of Israel is the **Tau/Ensign for the Last Lamb** of the Hebrews and the whole world which God showed to Abraham and Isaac in Mount Moriah. The foremost patriarchal father of the Jews by name Abraham offered two kinds of sacrifices on earth before his death. In each of the two sacrifices he offered, the Holy Ghost instructed him to do so. The commands to offer sacrifices came from the 'Great White Throne' whose	

interest Abraham represented. The first sacrifice was in Genesis 15:9, in which Abraham provided a heifer, a she- goat, a ram all of three years old, a turtledove and a young pigeon for the Most High. The second and last sacrifice was in Genesis 22. Here, God would not allow Abraham to come to Mount Moriah with any form of animal for sacrifice; neither would He allow him to hurt Isaac when He tested him. Instead, Yahweh/Jehovah would provide a 'Lamb' for Himself from heaven which Abraham would sacrifice in the presence of his son Isaac.

Abraham and Isaac were the only two people who witnessed the provision of a 'Divine Lamb' from heaven for sacrifice to Yahweh/Jehovah. They became the divine custodians of the mystery of Genesis 22 which is known as **'The Great Ensign'** of all ages. This is why the Psalmist, who wrote Psalm 119 by the Spirit of Yeshua/Jesus of Israel ended it with Tau; which is nd the 22 and last symbol or ensign of the mysteries of the Messiah. By the time of the revelation of the 'Last Lamb Mystery', Ishmael the son of Hagar was no longer living with Abraham and Sarah.

So, the Ishmaelites/Islams do not know the mystery of the 'Last Lamb' which God revealed to Abraham who is Yeshua/Jesus of Israel. great mystery. Then from Israel, it was handed over to the true prophets of Israel who held forth for the coming Yeshua/Jesus who is the purpose and overall embodiment of the mystery of the Aleph—Tau. On the Cross of Calvary, we see Yahweh/Jehovah/the Lord Yeshua/Jesus of Israel who is the promised and revealed Tau/Second and Last Lamb of the Father offering up Himself for the Hebrews and the world.

There on the Cross-, He gave Himself to be the final, complete, the ultimate and perfect sacrifice for the redemption of the souls of men from sin and Satan and for the liberation of His creation. Tau is the ensign for true perfection of the saints of God by the sacrifice of Christ. He has become the Last Lamb for the world. He is the 'Great Ensign' upon mount Calvary. His 'Atoning Precious Blood' is the 'Everlasting Ensign' that God commands all the Gentiles as well as the Jews to seek. His blood alone gives us access to the throne of glory. Yeshua/Jesus is our **'Great and Ancient Tau.'**

CHAPTER 11

THE PATRIARCHAL– SEQUENCIAL ORDER FROM ADAM TO ISRAEL IN CONNECTION WITH THE MYSTERY OF THE ALEPH—TAU

1	**Adam**	**Aleph** *Adam who was the first man from God knew that Yahweh/Jehovah the Father would one day send 'His Own Kind' who is the First and Only Begotten Son whose name is Yahweh/Jehovah the Son, to be the 'Great Seed' whose blood would be spilled for man's sins. Adam and Eve knew that Yeshua/Jesus the Messiah would be 'The First Born from the Dead' right from the day they sinned.
2	**Seth**	**Beth** *Seth who was the second person from Adam having been taught by his father, knew that Yahweh-kind or Jehovah-kind who is the 'Great Seed' of the woman/Abraham would be 'The House or Dwelling Place' on earth when He would come to redeem and reconnect His lost people back to Yahweh/Jehovah the Father.
3	Enosh	**Gimmel** *Enosh who was the third person from Adam knew that the 'Coming Great Seed' of the woman who is also called the 'Seed' of Abraham from heaven whose name is called Yeshua/Jesus of Israel/Nazareth would be 'The Merciful and Faithful One' to all.

4	Cainan	**Daleth** *Cainan who was the fourth person from Adam was taught that the 'Great Seed' of the woman/Abraham would be 'The Door/Gate/Way' out of hell and to heaven for all saints.
5	Mahalaleel	**Hey** *Mahalaleel who was the fifth person from Adam was taught that the promised 'Great Seed' of the woman/Abraham would be 'The Divine Pure Breath' that will restore the lost pure breath in man due to sin.
6	Jared	**Vau** *Jared who was the sixth person from Adam was taught that the 'Coming Great Seed' of the woman/Abraham would be 'The Re-connector/Reformer' of all the families of the earth and all things that were severed from heaven through sin.
7	Enoch	**Zayin** *Enoch who was the seventh person from Adam was taught that the 'Coming Great Seed' who is Yeshua/Jesus of Israel would be 'The Great Sword' that would slay Lucifer the great dragon that misleads man and be also the judge of all ungodly men. *"And Enoch also, the seventh from Adam, prophesied of these, saying, Behold, the Lord cometh with ten thousands of his saints, To execute judgment upon all, and to convince all that are ungodly among them of their ungodly deeds which they have ungodly committed, and of all their hard speeches which ungodly sinners have spoken against him"* (Jude 1:14).
8	Methuselah	**Chet** *Methuselah who was the eighth person from Adam was taught that the expected Messiah whose name is Yeshua/Jesus of Israel/Nazareth would be 'The Life' for all men and women. He is 'The Life' that gives life to all the dead. Methuselah was strongly connected to the **Chet**/Life from heaven that he lived 969 years.

9	Lamech	**Teth** *Lamech who was the ninth person from Adam was taught and assured that the 'Great Seed' of the woman/Abraham would be 'The Good One' or 'Goodness' that will sweep evil or the 'Evil One' away from the earth.
10	Noah	**Yodh** *Noah who was the tenth person from Adam was taught and assured that the 'Great Seed' of the woman/Abraham would be 'The Hand' that would rebuild all humanity destroyed by sin. *"And I also say unto thee, That thou art Peter, and upon this rock I will build my church; and the gates of hell shall not prevail against it"* (Matthew 16:18).
11	Shem	**Kaph** *Shem who was the eleventh person from Adam was taught and assured that this same 'Seed' would be 'The One Who Crowns' all the saints on the last day in heaven.
12	Arphaxad	**Lamed** *Arphaxad who was the twelfth person from Adam was taught that Yeshua/Jesus who is the 'Great Seed' would be 'The Wisdom/Purpose' of God for all men. He is the Supreme King for all. He was taught that the 'Coming Wisdom' is the principle thing or the 'Principal King' on earth.
13	Salah	**Mem** *Salah who was the thirteenth person from Adam was taught that this very 'Seed' of Abraham would be 'The Revealed One' or 'Revealed Messiah' of the whole world.
14	Eber	**Nun** *Eber who was the fourteenth person from Adam was taught that the 'Great Seed' that would come would be 'The Great Light/Brightness' that will enlighten everyone that comes into the world and also save us from gross darkness.
15	Peleg	**Samech** *Peleg who was the fifteenth person from Adam was taught that the 'Great Seed' would be 'The Divine Support/Protection' for all men.

16	Reu	**Ayin** *Reu who was the sixteenth person from Adam was taught that the 'Great Seed' would be 'The Eye' that runs back and forth the whole earth Who oversees and monitors all activities on earth.
17	Serug	**Pey** *Serug who was the seventeenth person from Adam was taught that the 'Great Seed' would be 'The Mouth' that would be the true advocate and intercessor for all people.
18	Nahor	**Tzaddik** *Nahor who was the eighteenth person from Adam was taught that the 'Great Seed' would be 'The Righteous/Just One' upon the earth by whom all would be justified and made righteous.
19	Terah	**Quf** *Terah who was the nineteenth person from Adam was taught that the 'Great Seed' would be the 'Holy One' upon the earth by whom holiness would be restored to humankind.
20	Abraham	**Resh/Rosh** *Abraham who was the twentieth person from Adam was taught that the 'Great Seed' would be 'The Supreme Head' of all things both in heaven and earth.
21	Isaac	**Schin** *Isaac who was the twenty-first person from Adam was taught that the 'Great Seed' that would come from Abraham would be 'The Peace, Power and Majesty' over all the earth.
22	Israel	**Tau** *Israel who was the twenty-second from Adam was taught that the 'Great Seed' would be 'The Last Sacrifice' to be made upon the earth for all people both Jews and Gentiles.

***Israel who is the twenty-second person from Adam and the second person from Abraham is the catchment centre for the true mysteries of Christ embodied in the Aleph-Tau. The Tau which exists at the level of Genesis 22, which is also the 'Cross of Yeshua/Jesus of Israel/Nazareth' in Jerusalem on Mount Moriah, during the 'Great Passover' in which the 'Great 'Seed' of Abraham was sacrificed is mysterious in nature. God who changed the requirements of sacrifices in Genesis 15 from a ram, a she-goat, an heifer, a turtle dove and a young pigeon, to a 'Divine Ram' from heaven in Genesis 22, had to change the 22nd and 2nd person from Adam and Abraham respectively,

from a natural name 'Jacob' to a divine name 'Israel.'
Genesis 15 is known as the 15 degree in the plane or realm of sacrifices while Genesis chapter 22 is nd known as the 22 and last degree of sacrifice. Genesis 15th degree is the operational realm of Levitical/Aaronic priesthood that offered animals from the earth as sacrifices to Yahweh/Jehovah while Genesis 22nd degree is the operational realm of the Messiah after the order of Melchizedek that offered a redemptive, reconciliatory and restorative sacrifice on the Cross of Calvary for the whole world. Abraham and Isaac migrated from Genesis 15 to Genesis 22 where they saw the Messianic Lamb of God. At the level of Genesis 22, Abraham saw no horror of darkness of any sort falling upon him as was the case in Genesis 15. Rather his son and he saw the glorious light that emanates from Mount Calvary through Christ's bloody sacrifice fall upon Isaac and himself.

All the orthodox Jews who still offer animal sacrifices are still operating under Genesis 15 with its great horrors of darkness. On the other hand, all the believers whose faith is in the blood of the Messianic Lamb of Abraham, Isaac and Israel who is Yeshua/Jesus of Israel/Nazareth are in the high planes of Genesis 22 which connects us directly to the throne of God with an amazing light. Genesis 15 does not take us to the throne of God. Genesis 22 is the only gateway to the throne of God because of the blood of Yeshua/Jesus our Messianic Lamb.

All the Jews who still offer animal sacrifices and still follow the Aaronic order instead of accepting the sacrificial death of Yeshua/Jesus of Israel in Jerusalem on Mount Moriah, are operating at the same level with the Islamic world who does not believe in Christ the 'Perfect and Last Sacrifice.' Moreover, the God of Abraham, Isaac and Israel has disannulled all sacrifices in the planes of Genesis 15 by His absolute sovereignty while at the same time upholding the 'Last Sacrifice' that was revealed to Abraham and Isaac in the planes of Genesis 22. Genesis 22 is the final plane of God which is Yeshua/Jesus of Israel/Nazareth the true and only Lamb for all who was offered in Jerusalem for the world. "For the priesthood being changed, there is made of necessity a change also of the law" (Hebrews 7:12).

The all-wise God who established the first priesthood in Genesis 15 through Abraham also used the same Abraham to establish the second and the final priesthood in Genesis 22. This is because God knew that the priesthood of

Genesis 15 that operates with animals' sacrifices would develop some faults with time so He took Abraham and his son Isaac who was a carrier of the divine oath of God to Mount Moriah to show them an everlasting priesthood and sacrifice.

"For finding fault with them, he saith, Behold, the days come, saith the Lord, when I will make a new covenant with the house of Israel and with the house of Judah: Not according to the covenant that I made with their fathers in the day I took them by the hand to lead them out of the land of Egypt; because they continued not in my covenant, and I regarded them not, saith the Lord" (Hebrews 8:8-9).

The Old Covenant revolves around Genesis 15 with the blood of animals that can never take away sins nor destroy demons while the New Covenant in the blood of Yeshua/Jesus that permanently removes sins from the souls of men and destroys demons and their powers, is deeply rooted in Genesis 22. "He hath remembered his covenant forever, the word which he commanded to thousand generations. Which covenant he made with Abraham, and his oath unto Isaac; and confirmed the same unto Jacob for a law, and to Israel for an everlasting covenant" (Psalm 105:9)

The Tau/the Last Lamb which God revealed to Abraham and Isaac on Mount Moriah, was confirmed to Israel who is the 22nd and 2nd person from Adam and Abraham respectively for an everlasting covenant. **The Aleph-Tau** which is the 'WORD' of Father revealed, which Yahweh/Jehovah the Father commanded to all generations has become:

*the covenant which God made with Abraham,
*the oath which God swore to Isaac,
*the law which God confirmed to Jacob and
*an everlasting covenant which God has established in Israel.

Unto Israel the faithful grandson of Abraham, the 'Great White Throne of God' committed the 22-mysteries of the Alep-Tau which solely belong to the Messiah the Prince. The Holy Ghost reveals the true meaning of the Aleph – Tau which sterns from the 'Great White Throne' only to the Jews and Gentiles who acknowledge that Yeshua/Jesus of Israel/Nazareth is the Son of the Living Father. Such people confess that Yeshua/Jesus was born in Bethlethem-Ephrathah, baptized in Jordan by John the Baptist, sacrificed for us on the Cross-in Jerusalem, buried in the tomb of Joseph of Arimathaea and raised up from the dead on the third day by the same Father Yahweh/Jehovah that sent Him. They also declare that He ascended bodily (not spiritually) to heaven and that He is coming back again to reclaim His earth.

CHAPTER 12

THE ERRORS AND CONSPIRACY OF THE ROMAN CATHOLIC CHURCH

Among the Roman Catholics, there is an impugned and erratic misuse of the Scriptures. They have distorted the Scriptures by attributing prophecies written concerning the 'Great Seed' from heaven to Mary. Spiritually, the Roman Catholics look contorted in shape because of their distortions of the Scriptures. One perfect example of such distortions of the Scriptures to support Catholic exaltation of Mary has to do with Genesis 3:15.

First, let us examine the true meaning of Genesis 3:15 by looking at the translation offered by all Protestant translators. In agreement with majority texts (MT) and the Greek Septuagint Old Testament (LXX), Protestant translations would render the passage in Genesis 3:15 as such, *"And I will put enmity between thee and the woman, and between thy seed and her seed; it shall bruise thy head, and thou shall bruise his feet"* (KJV)... *"I will put enmity between you and the woman, and between your offspring and her offspring; he shall bruise your head, and you shall bruise his heel"* (English Standard Version) ... *"I will put animosity between you and the woman, and between your descendant and her descendant; he will bruise your head, and you will bruise his heel"* (Complete Jewish Bible).

"He" in the original Hebrew is masculine and is pronounced "hoo" and can mean "it" in reference to King James Version. The word **"He"** in Genesis 3:15 should be understood as a Messianic prophecy about Yeshua/Jesus of Israel/Nazareth our Messiah who alone crushes the head of the serpent. However, Jerome (342-430 AD) in his Latin vulgate translation, made a major error by changing "it" or "He" into "she." The Roman Catholics in their **'DouayRheims Bible'** translated Genesis 3:15 as thus, *"I will put enmities between thee and the woman, and thy seed and her seed: she shall crush thy head, and thou shall lie in wait for her heel."* Instead of "He *shall crush your head"*, which refers solely to Yeshua/Jesus of Israel/Nazareth it becomes *"she shall crush your head"* referring to Mary.

The Roman Catholics just like Jehovah's Witness are in dire error indeed. From this mistranslation, they claim that instead of Yeshua/Jesus alone who crushed the head of the Satan through His death on the Cross; that it would be Mary, who would crush the head of Satan. They use this mistranslation to justify the doctrine of Immaculate Conception of Mary among other doctrines. Mary had a biological father and mother as well as a cousin by name Elizabeth. The fact that Mary was a virgin does not mean that she was sinless.

In December 2014, at Nnewi in Anambra state of Nigeria, I came across a Roman Catholic Christmas Rosary Crusade programme, titled, *"BEHOLD SHE THAT CRUSHES THE HEAD OF THE SERPENT"* (Genesis 3:15). This bill really caught up my attention and I became disgusted with their posts. To me it is one of the highest conspiracies against Yeshua/Jesus of Israel/Nazareth and the Holy Bible. From the pope to the least person who attend Roman Catholic Church and believe in their dogmas, all of them are in error. I call on all the true children of Yeshua/Jesus of Nazareth to stand gallantly and be veteran in defense of the name and person of our Saviour and God —Jesus Christ.

The Roman Catholics pray through Mary instead of praying through Jesus Christ who has crushed Satan through His death and whose blood accords us victory over the serpent. Mary can never crush the head of the serpent because she did not shed her blood. Moreover, the second reason she cannot do so is that she is not the ordained Lamb of God. We need to prove the Roman Catholics wrong by listening to the symphonic high praises accorded the Lamb of Calvary in the book of Revelation 5:7-12, *"And he came and took the book out of the right hand of him that sat upon the throne. And when he had taken the book, the four beasts and four and twenty elders fell down before the Lamb, having every one of them harps, and golden vials full of odours, which are the prayers of the saints.*

And they sung a new song, saying, Thou art worthy to take the book, and to open the seals thereof: for thou wast slain, and hath redeemed us to God by thy blood out of every kindred, and tongue, and people and nation; And hast made us unto our God kings and priests: and we shall reign on the earth."

REASONS WHY PEOPLE SHOULD NOT SEEK HELP FROM OR PRAY THROUGH MARY

- In verse 7, it is our Yahweh/Jehovah the Lamb of Calvary that came and took the book out of the right hand of our Father that sits upon the throne and

  not Mary. Mary does not have access to the right hand and throne of God. Only our Lamb does.
- In verse 8, all the four beasts and twenty-four elders fell down before the Lamb in adoration and not before Mary. It is an abomination among the four beasts and twenty-four elders and the entire community of angels to fall down before the person of Mary or her man- made image.
- In verse 9a, all the four beasts and twenty-four elders are raising their high and melodious symphonic song to the Lamb of God and not to Mary.
- To the Lamb of Calvary they are saying, *Thou art worthy to take the book and to open the seals thereof* and not to Mary. In chapters 6, 7 & 8, we see the crucified, buried, resurrected and ascended Lamb opening the seven seals of the book He took from the right hand of our Father and not Mary. Mary does not have the Father's book in her hand and can never open the seals.
- In verse 9b, all the four living beasts, twenty-four elders and community of innumerable angels are saying to our Lamb, *for thou wast slain* and not to Mary. Mary was not slain for anybody's sin. Only Yeshua/Jesus of Nazareth was slain in Jerusalem on the Cross of Calvary for the sins and forgiveness all men and women.
- In verse 9c, they say, *and hast redeemed us to God by thy blood out of every kindred, and tongue, and people and nation.* Only the Lamb of Calvary redeemed us unto God by His precious blood to God and not Mary. Mary does not redeem anybody because she is not the chosen Lamb of God. Again, she was not crucified on the Cross of Calvary. Moreover, her blood is not redemptive and therefore cannot redeem.
- In verse 10, the Lamb makes us kings and priests unto God the Father and not Mary. Mary does not have any authority and there is no investiture of power on her from God the Father to make any man priest and king on earth. Only the Lamb of God is eternally invested with such authority to make men and

women from every kindred, tongue, people and nation priests and kings unto our Father upon the throne.

In Hebrews 7:25, it is said of our Lord Yeshua/Jesus, *"Wherefore he is also able to save them to the utmost that come unto God by him, seeing he ever liveth to make intercession for them."*

- Only Master Yeshua/Jesus is able to save us to the utmost and not Mary.
- It is only by the Lord Jesus that we can come to God and not by Mary.
- It is only our Lord Yeshua/Jesus that ever lives and not Mary. Mary died just as every other saint did. Mary will resurrect by the power of the Lord Yeshua/Jesus on the last day.
- It is only Yeshua/Jesus that makes intercession for sinners and not Mary. Mary does not pray for anybody at all. Therefore, the Roman Catholic prayer of, *'Mary, mother of God please pray for us'* does not hold any substance before heaven and earth. It is eternally non–essential, invalid, unprofitable, useless and a total nonsense before God's throne.

WARNING TO THE WORLD

The Islamic World and other religions are the most offended when men and women declare that Yeshua/Jesus of Nazareth is Yahweh/Jehovah the Almighty God. The only reason Islam and other religions claim that the Bible is corrupt is simply because it speaks of the deity of Christ Jesus. They say they cannot bow down for 'the Man of Galilee.' As Mohammed and other religious leaders died in their sins and went to hell, so will all who follow Mohammed and other religions that oppose Yeshua/Jesus of Nazareth/Israel, die in their sins if they do not repent. All Islam and other religions are guilty of terrible sins of bloodshed. For example in every mosque, the foundation is laid with the blood of a fourteen year old virgin. Could it be because Mohammed did not have a single son that led him to postulate that Father Yahweh/Jehovah does not have a Son?

The Quran says in not less than eight places that when Adam was created, that God commanded all angels to bow and worship the man He had made. *"And we said to the angels, 'bow yourselves to Adam; they bowed themselves, save Iblis (Satan); he refused, and waxed proud, and became an unbeliever"* (Surah 2:34; 7:11f; 15:29-35; 17:61-62; 18:50; 20: 115ff and 38:71ff).

In other words, what made Iblis (Satan) an unbeliever was his refusal to bow for Adam. In Surah 15 and 38, God released some curses on Iblis for his arrogance. The question is: If the followers of Islam were on earth at that time would they too have bowed down for Adam? Moreover, would not that be un-Islamic? That is an axe for them to grind.

THE DEITY OF YESHUA/JESUS UNVEILED

The purpose of our Lord Yeshua/Jesus did not become clear to the disciples until after His resurrection, and the revelation of His 'Deity' consequent thereon. Thomas, when he realized the significance of the presence of a 'mortal wound' in the body of a living man, immediately joined with it the absolute title of Deity, saying, *"My Lord, and my God"* (John 20:28). The term, 'My Lord and my God' is only applied to Yahweh the Father and Yahweh His Son, *"Praising God, and having favour with all the people. And the Lord added to the church daily such as should be saved"* (Acts 2:47). *"And now, Lord, behold their threatening: and grant unto thy servants, that with boldness they may speak thy word. By stretching thy hand to heal, and that signs and wonders may be done in the name of thy holy child Jesus"* (Acts 4:29-30).

How soon and how completely the lower meaning of the word 'Lord' had been superseded is seen in Peter's declaration in his first sermon after His resurrection, *"Therefore let all the house of Israel know assuredly that God hath made that same Jesus(Yeshua/Salvation of Israel), whom ye have crucified, both Lord and Christ"* (Acts 2:36, Emphasis Mine). Also in the house of Cornelius, our brother Peter made another declaration of the 'Deity' of Yeshua/Jesus of Nazareth, *"The word which God sent unto the children of Israel, preaching peace by Jesus Christ: (he is Lord of all)"* (Acts 10:36). To consolidate the veracious claims that our heavenly Father and His Son share all things together let us once again study the following chart.

THE FATHER AND THE SON ARE ONE

Matthew 11:25	Acts2:36;10:36;17:24 and Revelation 17:14
"At that time Jesus answered and said, I thank thee, O Father, Lord of heaven and earth, because thou hast hid these things from the wise and prudent, and hast revealed them unto babes." Commentary: In the above Scripture, the Son of Yahweh/Jehovah the Father called His own very Father, *"Lord of heaven and earth."*	*"Therefore let all the house of Israel know assuredly, that God hath made that same Jesus, whom you crucified both Lord and Christ"... "The word which God sent unto the children of Israel, preaching peace by Jesus Christ: (he is Lord of all)"... "God that made the world and all things therein, seeing that he is Lord of heaven and earth, dwelleth not in temples made with hands"... "And they shall make war with the Lamb, and the Lamb shall overcome them: for he is the Lord of lords and King of kings: and they that are with him are called, and chosen, and faithful."* Commentary: From apostles Peter, Paul and John who preached these sermons in Acts 2:36 and 10:36; Acts 17:24 and Revelation 17:14 respectively, it has been established that Yahweh the Son who is Yeshua/Jesus of Israel is the Lord of all—heaven and earth just as our Father Yahweh is the Lord of heaven and earth according to Matthew 11:25.

APPLICATIONS OF THE OLD TESTAMENT TO YESHUA/JESUS IN THE NEW TESTAMENT

In Peter's writing, the implication of his early teachings are confirmed and developed. Thus Psalm 34:8, *"O taste and see that the LORD/Yahweh/Jehovah is good: blessed is the man that trusteth in him"* is solely applied to our Lord Jesus and in 1Peter 2:3, the prophecy in Psalm 34:8 becomes, *"If so be ye have tasted that the Lord is gracious."* Then, the prophecy in Isaiah 8:13, which says, *"Sanctify the LORD (Yahweh/Jehovah) of hosts himself; and let Him be your fear, and let him be your dread,"* becomes *"Sanctify in your hearts Christ as Lord"* (1Peter 3:15a, Emphasis Mine). All the disciples were together in the same place, time and day when Thomas said to our Master Jesus, *'My Lord and my God.*

THE FIRST ADAM ANDJESUS CHRIST THE SECOND ADAM

1 Corinthians 15: 45a and 47a	1 Corinthians 15:45b and 47 b
"And so it is written, The first man Adam was made a living soul"... "The first man is of the earth, earthy."	"The *last Adam was made a quickening spirit" ... "The second man is the Lord from heaven."*

Who is the second Adam? Where did He come from? What is His name? For us to understand this statement, *"The second man is the Lord from heaven,"* we need to understand the core-relation between the "LORD" and the "Lord" in the Old and New Testaments.

Joel 2:32 and Deuteronomy 6:16	**Acts 2:21 and Matthew 4:7**
"And it shall come to pass that whosoever shall call on the name of the LORD (Yahweh/Jehovah) shall be delivered: for in mount Zion and in Jerusalem shall be deliverance, as the LORD hath said, and in the remnant whom the LORD shall call." "Ye shall not tempt the LORD (Yahweh/Jehovah) your God, as ye tempted him in Massah."	** *"And it shall come to pass, that whosoever shall call upon the Lord shall be saved"*** ***"Jesus said unto him, It is written again, thou shalt not tempt the Lord thy God."*** From the book of Genesis to Malachi, the name of Yahweh/Jehovah who created all things, translated as 'LORD',

	is the same Yahweh/Jehovah that has been translated and written as 'Lord' in the New Testament. In Joel 2:32, it says, *"And whosoever shall call on the name of the LORD/Yahweh/Jehovah shall be delivered"* and then in Acts 2:21 it says, *"And it shall come to pass, that whosoever shall call upon the Lord/Yahweh/Jehovah shall be saved"* (Emphasis Mine).

THE ERRORS AND CONSPIRACY OF THE ROMAN CATHOLIC CHURCH

In Deuteronomy 6:16, the same LORD/Yahweh/Jehovah is translated as 'Lord' in Matthew 4:7. Then, in 1Corinthians 15:47b, it says, *"The second man is the Lord from heaven"* The uncontroversial core-relation between both Testaments is that the very Person called the LORD/Yahweh/Jehovah in the O.T. is same Person called the 'Lord' in the N.T. Therefore, the 'Second Man/Adam from Heaven' who is Yeshua/Jesus of Israel/Nazareth is the Lord/LORD/Yahweh/Jehovah the Son of Yahweh/Jehovah the Father.

DO ANGELS HAVE A FATHER?

"How art thou fallen from heaven, O Lucifer son of the morning! How art thou cut down to the ground, which didst weaken the nations!" (Isaiah 14:12). *"When the morning stars sang together, and all the sons of God shouted for joy"* (Job 38:7).

Here, we see that Lucifer is called the son of the morning. The questions we must ask ourselves are: What does the son of the morning mean and whose name is called the 'Morning' in the Bible whose son Lucifer was? *"I Jesus sent mine angel to testify unto you these things in the churches. I am the root and the offspring of David, and the bright and morning star"* (Revelation 22:16). Since Lucifer is called the son of the morning in Isaiah 14:12, it means that his Father and Creator is Yeshua/Jesus of Israel/Nazareth the Bright and Morning Star. Angel Michael, angel

Gabriel, angel Lucifer and other billions of angels who are called 'morning stars,' have the same Father and Creator. They are known as the sons of the 'Morning' or the sons of the Bright and Morning Star' who is Yeshua/Jesus the Everlasting Father.

Therefore, when the Islamic world say that God does not have a Son, they are only telling lies. Out of the several billions of angels that worship the Son of God, Lucifer/Allah/Iblis and his angelic group who are now called demons or jinns, became the only group that refused to worship the Lord/LORD/Yahweh/Jehovah from heaven who is Yeshua/Jesus of Israel/Nazareth the second Adam.

WHO DID YAHWEH/JEHOVAH THE FATHER COMMAND ALL ANGELS TO WORSHIP?

"And again when he bringeth in the first-begotten into the world, he saith, And let all the angels of God worship him" (Hebrews 1:6). *"Then saith Jesus unto him, Get thee hence, Satan: for it is written, Thou shalt worship the Lord thy God and him only shalt thou serve"* (Matthew 4:10). In John 3:16 our Lord/LORD/Yahweh/Jehovah from heaven is called God's only begotten

Son and in Hebrews 1:6, He is called God's first-begotten Son. From God's 'First and Only–Begotten Son', came forth into existence all angels and human beings.

When the absolute order came from the 'Almighty Invisible Father' that all the angels of God should worship His 'First and Only Begotten Son' whom He brought into the world, all the angels obeyed the voice of the Father except Lucifer/Allah/Iblis and the angels with him. Then in Jude 1:6, the Father commanded His Son who is the 'Second Adam/Man' from heaven to bind those disobedient angels with everlasting chains and reserve them in darkness until the judgment of the great day.

The commandment of the Father for all the angels to worship His 'First and Only–Begotten Son' from heaven is an absolute decree for all angels and men. All the Islamic world, Jews and the people of the world who refuse to worship Yeshua/Jesus of Israel/ Nazareth who is the Lord/LORD/Yahweh/Jehovah from heaven whom the Father sent forth to redeem and ransom the race of the first Adam from Satan/Iblis, will face the wrath of the Almighty Father in the darkness of hell fire.

When Lucifer/Iblis the fallen angel who Mohammed and the Islamic religion call 'Allah' appeared to Mohammed, he said that he was angel Gabriel. Mohammed who claimed to be the apostle of Allah said in the Hadith 5:266, *"By Allah (I swear), though I am the Apostle of Allah, yet I do not know what Allah will do to me."*

Is it wise for Islamic community to follow a man who tells us that he is the greatest prophet and the seal of the messengers of God yet does not know whether he is going to the Paradise he is preaching about? Mohammed was a man of uncertainties until his death. The Islamic world preaches that only those who die in Jihad will enter into Paradise. Unfortunately, Mohammed did not die as a Jihadist. He died in his house from the poison he took from a Jewish woman whose husband he had killed. To every Islamic nation, Yeshua/Jesus of Israel *offers eternal certainty as thus, "I came forth from the Father, and am come into the world: again, I leave the world, and go to the Father"* (John 16:28)... *"Jesus knowing that the Father had given all things into his hands, and that he was come from God and went to God"* (John 13:3). Both Mohammed and all the uncountable billions of men and women who follow Islam that died without the LORD/Lord/Yahweh/Jehovah/the Son who is Yeshua/Jesus of Israel/Nazareth are forever lost in hell fire. All the Jews who died without Yeshua/Jesus Christ are also lost in hell fire. All who do not follow the Son of God who is Yahweh/Jehovah from heaven who has come in human form for our deliverance from Satan and hell, will definitely follow Lucifer (Allah/Iblis) and his demons to everlasting fire in hell.

BY WHOM DO ANGELS SWEAR?

Revelation 10:6	Colossians 1:16	Genesis 1:1
*"And sware by him that liveth forever and ever, who **created** heaven, and the things therein are, the earth, and the things therein are, and the sea, and the things which are therein, that there should be time no longer"*	*"For by him were all things created, that are in heaven and that are in earth, visible and invisible, whether they be thrones, or dominions, or principalities, or powers: all things were **created** by him, and for him"*	*"In the beginning, God **created** the heaven and earth"*

All the holy angels swear by Him that created all things and this Person is the Lord Yeshua/Jesus of Nazareth. The true prophets and apostles of God testify that Yeshua/Jesus is Yahweh the Creator. In the chapters and verses of the Scriptures above, the word 'created' is used to refer to the works of our Lord Yeshua/Jesus.

YESHUA/JESUS THE GIVER OF POWER TO ISRAEL

The bonding and networking between the Old and New Testament Scriptures are profound. Once more, let us study and meditate upon the revealed word of God in the chart below.

In Deuteronomy 8:18, the Bible called on all the Israelites to remember the *LORD/Lord/Yahweh/Jehovah their God who gave their fathers power to get wealth.* Then in Luke 10:19, the Lord Jesus our Messiah said, *Behold I give unto you power to tread upon scorpions and serpents and over all the power of the enemy.* *"Hear, O Israel: the LORD our God is one"* (Deuteronomy 6:4)... *"And Jesus answered him, The first of all the commandments is, Hear, O Israel; the Lord our God is one Lord"* (Mark 12:29). Since the LORD/Lord/Yahweh/Jehovah of Israel is one Lord, this implies that there is only one Person that gives them power to get wealth and tread upon scorpions and serpents and this 'One Person' is the Lord/LORD/Yahweh/Jehovah Yeshua/Jesus of Israel/Nazareth our Messiah.

He is the only power giver to Abraham, Isaac, Israel and their descendants. From the books of Genesis to Malachi and from Malachi to Revelation, there ***'Only*** **One Power Giver' to humanity and this Person is ou**r Yahweh/Jehovah/LORD/Lord and Saviour Yeshua/Jesus of Nazareth. This prophecy is the most important prophecy in the Holy Bible. The message says to all the Israelites in all the nations of the world that Yeshua/Jesus of Nazareth/Israel is the *'Only One God and Saviour'* of Israel and the whole world. Therefore, we are called to love, serve, and worship, seek after and follow Him with our whole heart, soul and might.

CHAPTER 13

THE REAL COMMONWEALTH OF ISRAEL AS WRITTEN AND REPORTED BY APOSTLE PAUL

"Wherefore remember, that ye being in time past Gentiles in the flesh, who are called Uncircumcision by that which is called the Circumcision in the flesh made by hands; That at that time ye were without Christ, being aliens from the commonwealth of Israel, and strangers from the covenant of promise, having no hope, and without God in the world" (Ephesians 2:11-12).

The high point that Apostle Paul stressed in verse 12 is *'alienation of the Gentiles from the commonwealth of Israel'*. We would like to define what commonwealth is. Commonwealth comprises two root words namely, "common" which means "belonging to all" and "wealth" meaning "happiness, riches, power, or joy." For us to have a clearer understanding of Ephesians 2:11-12, we are going to read this verse in another Bible translation:

"Therefore, remember your former state: you Gentiles by birth—called Uncircumcision by those who, merely because of an operation on their flesh, are called the Circumcision— at that time had no Messiah. You were estranged from the national life of Israel. You were foreigners to the covenants embodying God's promise. You were in this world without hope and without God" (Complete Jewish Bible).

From these two translations based on *'King James Version* and *Complete Jewish Bible'*, another word for the **'Commonwealth of Israel'** is the **'National Life of Israel.'** If we are going to transform our cities and nations, we must give utmost attention to what the Bible calls the *'Commonwealth of Israel or the National Life of Israel.'* Apostle Paul was a man chosen by the Holy Ghost (Ruach HaKodesh) to be a teacher of the Word of God to both the Jews and Gentiles. He made all men and women understand that there is **'One National Life'** of Israel. He worked with the

Holy Ghost to call the Gentiles who were aliens to the National Life of Israel to come and share with the people of Israel, their National Life.

The interesting question we must ask ourselves is: 'what is the Commonwealth or the National Life of Israel?' What is it that makes Israel happy, glad and rich that every person in Israel is required to give a professional pursuit and carrier throughout his lifetime?

THE REAL COMMON SALVATION OF ISRAEL AS WRITTEN AND REPORTED BY APOSTLE JUDE

For us to understand this in depth, let us consider the writing of Apostle Jude whose writing holds and reveals deep mysteries. *"Beloved, when I gave all diligence to write unto you of the common salvation, it was needful for me to write unto you, and exhort you that you should earnestly contend for the faith which was once delivered unto the saints"*(Jude 1:3).

As our brother, Jude gave all diligence to write to the saints, his main or most primary focus was on the **'Common Salvation or Common Yeshua/Jesus.'** What Apostle Paul by the Holy Ghost called the **'Commonwealth of Israel'** in Ephesians 2:12 is what Apostle Jude by the same Spirit of truth calls the **'Common Salvation'** or **'Common Yeshua/Jesus of Israel.'** When this 'Divine Being' called Yeshua in Hebraic language appeared to the biological father of the twelve tribes of Israel, an everlasting covenant was cut between God Almighty and Israel and his offspring in all generations.

The term of that covenant is that from the time the covenant was made between God and our father Israel, the **'Salvation/Yeshua/Jesus'** of Israel" would henceforth be known as **'the Commonwealth or Common Salvation'** of all the twelve tribes of Israel and their children.' This ***"Common Salvation/Yeshua/Jesus or Commonwealth of Israel'*** belongs to everyone and He is commonly called the God of Israel. He is like an endless sea that satisfies everyone's need. This very knowledge of the ***'Common Salvation/Yeshua/Jesus of Israel'*** that the Holy Ghost inspired Jude to write about is what the Bible also calls the 'Common Faith' of the fathers of Israel and all who believe Yeshua/Jesus. The Holy Ghost through the epistle of Brother Jude commands us to earnestly aver and contend for this very faith in the "Common Salvation/Yeshua/Jesus or Commonwealth of Israel". Our Lord Jesus Christ is the real Commonwealth of Israel and for all the nations. So, from

Ephesians 2:12 and Jude 1:3, we have these settings, "**The Commonwealth of Israel" = "The Common Salvation" ⇒ Common Yeshua ⇒ Common Jesus of Israel/ Nazareth."**

THE SUPERIOR COMMONWEALTH

The 'Real Commonwealth or National Life of Israel' according to the Scriptures is our awesome Saviour and Lord Yeshua/Jesus of Nazareth the only Christ. He is much more superior to the commonwealth of the nations. He is the ***'Real National Life of Israel'*** (RNLI) or the ***'Real Commonwealth of Israel'*** (RCI).

The British and American Commonwealth of nations and every other national life of any nation are a lesser life. The most mind- burgling question we must ask ourselves again is this: since it has been proved Scripturally from Ephesians 2:12 and Jude 1:3 that our Master and Lord Yeshua/Jesus is the **'Real National Life of Israel', then,** who or what is the Commonwealth i.e. national life of Britain, America, the Germans or the entire Gentile nations? Again, since the **'Commonwealth or National Life of Israel'** is a Person and not a phenomenon, the question before us is: who is that person that the Americans, the British people, and other nations call their Commonwealth or national life? If Yeshua/Jesus of Nazareth is not your nation's *National Life*, then, possibly Satan is.

THE BLESSED NATION

As the Psalmist says in Psalm 33:12, "*Blessed is the nation whose God is the LORD; and the people whom he hath chosen for his own inheritance;* so do I say to all nations of the earth. "*Blessed is the nation whose Commonwealth or Real National Life is Yeshua/Jesus of Israel/Nazareth who is our Messiah the Prince.*" All the Messianic Community (Churches of Christ) is blessed because Yeshua/Jesus has become our *'Real Commonwealth' or 'Real National and Community Life'* as He said in John 14:6. Anybody, movements, governments or organizations that do not have the *'Commonwealth or the Real National Life of Israel'* is not blessed no matter how industrialized and technologically strong they may appear to be. Industrialization and technologies do not mean blessedness. Rather such nations that are without Yeshua/Jesus at all are under the curse of the Almighty God. We, who belong to Yeshua/Jesus, must seek partnership with the power of the Holy

Ghost for us to restore to the people in our nations the ***'Real National Life of Israel.'***

We must fight the good fight of the faith and earnestly contend for it until Yeshua/Jesus of Nazareth the Son the living God is enthroned and established at all levels in our nations to become the 'Real National/Community Life for all people.'

THE ENDURING PRIMARY GOAL OF YESHUA/JESUS OF ISRAEL

The primary works of our Lord Yeshua/Jesus is clearly detailed and defined throughout the Old Testament prophesies. Angel Gabriel visited each of the prophets that spoke about the imminent coming of the Lord Jesus just as he visited Zechariah the father of John the Baptist. He also made this known to Joseph in his dream, *"And she shall bring forth a son, and thou shall call his name JESUS: for he shall save his people from their sin"* (Mathew 1:21).

God created humanity pure, but as the enemy came against man, he introduced sin into man's life. In Genesis3:1, Satan appeared as a serpent in order to deceive man. **After leading the first pure couple astray into doing 'his own will,'** he also

appeared to Cain in the person of sin. *"If thou doest not well, sin lieth at the door. And unto thee shall be his desire, and thou shall rule over him"* **(Genesis4:9).**

Satan has always sought how to invade humanity by transforming himself in different forms. The form in which he appeared to Adam and Eve was not the same form in which he appeared to Cain. As he appeared to Adam and Eve, he became the ***"Serpent."*** To Cain, he became **"Sin"** at the door of Cain's heart.

The book of Isaiah exposed Lucifer as he is. *"In that day, the LORD with his sore, and great and strong sword shall punish leviathan the piercing serpent and even leviathan that cooked serpent and he will slay the dragon that is in the sea"* (Isaiah 27:1). The split personality of Lucifer is that he is called both *'Leviathan the piercing serpent, Leviathan the cooked serpent and the Dragon in the sea'* or in people.

When Adam and Eve were attacked in the Garden of Eden, it was actually Leviathan and the Dragon in the sea that initiated that onslaught. Leviathan and the Dragon is one person. Lucifer the fallen angel was once called son of the Morning Star. So, let us interlock, Genesis 3:1 and Isaiah 27:1 expansively for deeper insight into the battle against humanity.

FIRST SEGMENT

"Now the serpent (Leviathan the piercing serpent, Emphasis Mine) was more subtle than any beast of the field..." "Now the serpent (the Dragon that is in the sea) was more than any beast of the field which the LORD God had made.

SECOND SEGMENT

"And he (Leviathan the piercing serpent) said unto the woman..." (Genesis 3:1) ... *"And he (Leviathan the crooked serpent) said unto the woman..."* (Genesis 3:1). *"And he (the Dragon that is in the sea) said unto the woman..."* (Genesis 3:1). The balancing of the Scriptures tells us the rank of the fallen angel that led this invasion of deception against the pure race of Adam. Round about Leviathan the piercing serpent, Leviathan the crooked serpent and the Dragon in the sea, were other fallen angels in the Garden of Eden placed by Satan as expeditionary forces against Adam and Eve. As Leviathan whose profile is detailed in Job 41:1end, succeeded in deceiving, displacing and dethroning man through his lies, he released his demonic expeditionary forces to fill the earth instead of the first Adam and his offspring. Satan who is also the Leviathan and the Dragon in the sea attempted a very strong assault on Cain in the day of sacrifice. In that very day, he appeared in the person of **'Sin.'** Around him in the field where Cain and Abel went to sacrifice, were those expeditionary forces of demons that had been made sins by Satan the **'Sin.'**

In Genesis 4:7 God defined Satan as 'Sin' and his demons as 'sins.' When humanity fell from God's order and began to follow Satan who is **'Sin'** and his demons who are **'sins'** personified, men and women became known as 'sinners' or followers of 'sins'. Sinners are God's original people who 'Sin (Satan) and sins (demons)' have deceived into believing and living in rebellion against their good God even Yeshua/Jesus.

Satan who is the very 'Sin' that God spoke about in Genesis 4:7, at the fall of man placed his loyal 'sins' (demons) around and against God's people. Sin (Satan) empowers his 'sins' (demons) to make men and women sinners. So, the all-time primary millennial goal of our blessed Redeemer, the Lord Yeshua/Jesus is to save

His people from their sins or numerous demons that Satan has released, attached to and set against every man and woman.

DEMONS ARE GATE–WAYS TO ALL SINS

"And she said, no man, Lord. And Jesus said unto her, Neither do I condemn thee: go and sin no more" (John8:11). Our sister, Mary Magdalene was a sinner bound by sins (demons) of fornication, adultery and other vices. In many cases, **'Sin'** (Satan) had ordered and released his 'sins' (demons) against her to lure her into fornication which violated God's lawful commandment in Exodus 20:14. This states, *"Thou shall not commit adultery."* Up against this woman were strong demons that ***'Sin'*** had placed in her way to lead her to act against God's word.

Our Lord Jesus did not just tell Mary Magdalene to go and sin no more, rather He took responsibility of her deliverance as the Scriptures said. *"Now when Jesus was risen early the first day of the week, he appeared first to Mary Magdalene, out of whom he had cast out seven devils"* (Mark 16:9). The Lord Jesus came to save Mary Magdalene from her sins and her sins were those seven devils that bound themselves with her soul unto adultery and other vices.

The book of Revelation states, *"And he laid hold on the dragon (the Dragon in the sea), that old serpent (Leviathan the piercing serpent and Leviathan the crooked serpent), which is the Devil, and Satan, and bound him a thousand years"* (Revelation 20:2, Emphasis mine).

The devil that is the head of all the devils sets his devils (sins) against every individual. Therefore, when we say that Christ came to save His people from their sins, it means that he came to save us from the demons that drag us into disobedience to God's word and every good thing. For instance, there are demons responsible for adultery, idolatry, smoking, fighting, wars, anger, witchcraft, etc.

CHAPTER 14

PRAYER OF DELIVERANCE FROM SINS (DEMONS)

"Saying, Let us alone; what have we to do with thee, thou Jesus of Nazareth? Art thou come to destroy us? I know thee who thou art; the Holy One of God" (Luke 4:34).

The primary reason our Lord Jesus Christ has come forth from the Father into the world is to destroy all the 'sins' (devils/demons) that have been employed and empowered by ***'Sin'*** to destroy humanity. Our Saviour and Lord Yeshua/Jesus accomplished the destruction of 'Sin'—the Devil and his fellow devils through His death on the Cross of Calvary. *"For as much as the children are partakers of flesh and blood, he also himself likewise took part of the same; that through death he might destroy him that had the power of death, that is the devil; And deliver them who through the fear of death were all their lifetime subject to bondage"* (Hebrews 2:14-15).

From the birth of Christ throughout the time of his ministry, He only rebuked and cast away demons. He did not destroy anyone of them until His death on the Cross of Calvary in Jerusalem. The destruction of the devil and all his devils took place on the Cross of Calvary through the sacrificial death of Yeshua/Jesus of Israel/Nazareth. The death of our Saviour Jesus who saves us from our sins (demons) destroyed all the demons in order to deliver us from fear of death.

His death is the weapon of mass destruction against all demons. As He destroyed those demons, humanity was saved from their sins. For us to experience in reality this marvelous deliverance from all demons, we must acclaim, activate and appropriate the Lamb's death upon our lives and homes. We must pray the right prayers based on the death of Yeshua/Jesus our Lord. *"For what the law could not do, in that it was weak through the flesh, God sending his son in the likeness of sinful flesh, and for sin, condemned sin in the flesh"* (Romans 8:3).

Remember according to John 3:17 that God did not send His Son Yeshua/Jesus to condemn the world. Rather He sent Him into the world to condemn 'Sin' (Satan) and all 'sins' (demons). It is quite certain that once an object or a criminal has been condemned legally that it is subject to destruction. The analogy here shows the condition of 'Sin' (Satan/Iblis/Allah) and all the sins (demons) who invaded humanity. When those demons invaded humanity, they began to take possession of human bodies originally designed by our Lord Yeshua/Jesus and made for the Holy Spirit.

The deliverance ministry of our Lord Yeshua/Jesus focuses on casting out those sins (demons) from our flesh. He would first condemn 'Sin' (Satan) in the flesh and then destroy him and his demons out of our bodies.

GUIDELINES FOR PRAYER OF CONDEMNING AND DESTROYING SIN AND DEVILS IN OUR BODIES

The sins or the demons that desire to control our flesh are listed in Galatians 5:19. We are going to pray the prayers of the death of Christ in dealing with them. Before you begin to pray, first proclaim Galatians 2:20 as thus, *"I am crucified with Christ: nevertheless I live; yet not I, but Christ liveth in me: and the life which I now live in the flesh I live by the faith of the Son of God; who loved me and gave himself for me."* The real spiritual condition of every man is either Christ living in him as He lived in Apostle Paul and other Apostles or that sins (demons) are living in him. If you desire for Christ to live in you, then follow these pattern of prayers:

1. Oh Holy Spirit, I desire to be crucified with Christ.
2. Let the death of Christ on His Cross permeate through my spirit, soul and body (SSB) and destroy all the hidden sins (demons) within me.
3. According to Romans 8:3, I join my Saviour Yeshua/Jesus to condemn sins (demons) in my flesh.
4. By the death of Christ, I condemn Satan and his demons in my flesh saying that my flesh is not for you but for the Holy Ghost.
5. Having condemned you, I embrace the glorious destructive death of my Lord Yeshua/Jesus on the Cross-to destroy the devil and his devils out of my spirit soul and body.
6. According to 1 Corinthians 11:26, I am commanded to proclaim the death of the Lord Yeshua/Jesus until He comes, therefore I proclaim that the Lord

Jesus through His death has destroyed the devil and his devils that had the power of death over my flesh.

7. By the death of the Lord Yeshua/Jesus, I allow the Holy Ghost to destroy all the works of the devil in my spirit, soul and body (SSB).
8. Lord Jesus, release the explosive power of your death through my spirit, soul and body (SSB) to destroy these sins that invaded my "SSB" according to Galatians 5:19-21.
9. I cry to the Holy Spirit to manifest the works of the death of our Lord Yeshua/Jesus in my "SSB" to destroy adultery, fornication, uncleanness, lasciviousness, idolatry and witchcraft, which I inherited from my paternal and maternal lineages.
10. Holy Spirit magnify in my "SSB" the death of the Lord Jesus/Yeshua by which He destroyed the devil and his works, to unleash perpetual destruction against the sins or demons of hatred, variance, emulation, wrath, strife, sedition and heresies in my heart and mind.
11. Lord Jesus by faith I travel through the high ways of your dreaded death on the Cross of Calvary to experience total liberation from the sins of envying, murders, drunkenness, reveling, unrighteousness, wickedness and covetousness which bound my SSB for years.
12. Abba Father as you accomplished the salvation of the saints through the sacrificial death of the Lamb on the Cross, I expose my whole "SSB" to the awesome death of Christ to destroy all the nature of the devil in me, namely the sins of maliciousness, debate, deceit, malignity, whispering, backbiting, hatred against God.
13. Let the death of Christ prevail through my "SSB" to destroy the sins of being despiteful to people, pride, boasting, invention of evil things, disobedience to biological and spiritual parents, breaking of covenants and unmerciful attitudes.
14. Eternal Holy Spirit I allow you to strip my "SSB" of every 'will of demons' placed therein that stands against the will of God for my life.
15. Let the old nature or old man which is equally the nature of the old serpent that deceived man in Eden be completely broken off my "SSB."
16. I release my "SSB" to God the builder of all things to rebuild, cleanse, purify, revive, enlighten, empower and refurbish them with the divine nature of God the Father, God the Son and God the Holy Spirit.
17. Holy Spirit, I call on you to invest the glorious works of our Lord Yeshua/Jesus in my "SSB" now that you have destroyed the works of the devil.

18. Holy Spirit I willingly yield my "SSB" to the Spirit, Soul and Body of the Lord Yeshua/Jesus for His glorious use and for your habitation.
19. Holy Spirit, please convert my "SSB" to become a house of prayer for all nations.
20 Fill this temple (my SSB) with your glory and love once again.

CHAPTER 15

THE SALVATION OF ISRAEL AND THE JEWISH PEOPLE

It is by the words and power of Yeshua/Jesus of Nazareth our Mashiach/Christ that Israel, Jerusalem and Judah have been preserved until date. He is the Holy One of Israel revealed in the Bible from Genesis to Malachi. He is the only God and King of Israel. His ruling over Israel His beloved nation is eternal. His Word over Israel is final and irrevocable.

We must understand that the longest exile of Israel as a nation that started in 70AD to 1948AD was prophesied by the "Salvation/Yeshua/Jesus of Israel" according to the book of Luke, *"However when you see Yerushalayim (Jerusalem) surrounded by armies, then you are to understand that she is about to be destroyed. Those in Y'hudah (Judah) must escape to the hills, those inside the city must get out, and those in the country must not enter it. For these are the days of vengeance when everything that has been written in the Tanakh will come true. What a terrible time it will be for pregnant women and nursing mothers! For there will be great distress in the Land and judgment on the people. Some will fall by the edge of the sword, others will be carried into all the countries of the Goyim (Gentiles), and Yerushalayim will be trampled down by the Goyim until the age of the Goyim has run its course"* (Luke 21:20-24, Complete Jewish Bible).

Just as the Psalmist desired that the ***Salvation/Yeshua/Jesus of Israel*** would come out of Zion during the days of their return from captivity, their **Salvation/Yeshua/Jesus** has indeed shown Himself faithful to Israel in order to help the offspring of the Hebrew patriarchs in all their distresses from 66AD until date. By the power and faithfulness of Yeshua/Jesus, He has preserved Israel and this should cause Israel as a nation to rejoice in Yeshua/Jesus HaMashiach/the Messiah our King. Even the atheists among the people believed that there was a supernatural hand that delivered Israel from over 2000 years of captivity and their subsequent trials and pains.

In 1897, Dr. Theodore Herzl convened the first International Zionist conference in Basal, Switzerland. By this, he officially birthed the Zionist movement among the Jewish people. Prophetically, this is what he recorded in his diary in his hotel room, *"today I created the Jewish State."* At the very point of the creation of the state of Israel, the ***"Salvation/Yeshua/Jesus of Israel"*** was present to cause the awakening as the Prophet Joel foresaw and declared. He said, *"Proclaim ye among the Gentiles; Prepare war, wake up the mighty men, let all the men of war draw near; let them come up: Beat your plowshares into swords, and your pruning hooks into spears: let the weak say I am strong"* (Joel 3:9-10).

Yeshua/Jesus of Israel manifested one of His wonders in the restoration of the Hebrew language and script. During the period of over 2000 years of the Jewish captivity across many nations of the world, the Hebrew language was as good as dead. Only the rabbis and teachers spoke it and this was only during religious ceremonies and observations. However, during the early years of the 20th century, parallel to the increased migration of Jewish pioneers into the land, a man named Eliezer Ben-Yahuda set himself single handedly to restore the ancient Hebrew tongue. This man and his family suffered so much mockery and persecution in the hand of fellow Jews as he insisted that his family speak only the Hebrew language. At this time of reformation of the Hebrew dialect, the **Salvation/Yeshua/Jesus** of Israel was present to cause the restoration of the original language and script.

Prior to the 1948 Israel's Independence, the British government delivered the region from the Moslem Turkish Empire that was by nature hostile to the purpose of God. Dr Weizmann, a Jewish scientist serving the British defense department, gained England's gratitude for his wartime invention of a new explosive that turned the tide against the Germans during World War 1. When asked for recompense he responded, *"I ask for a national home for my people in their ancient homeland"* In every feat achieved by the Jews, the **Salvation/Yeshua/Jesus** of Israel was present to help His own people. Moreover, England granted his request and commissioned by the League of Nations to administrate Palestine in preparation for the establishment of a Jewish State.

The **Salvation/Yeshua/Jesus** of Israel was present to fight for Israel during the six days' war of 1967. From the Egyptian and Syrian fronts came hostile armies but Israel had strategically wanted to keep the long eastern front with Jordan aggression free. They even sent a letter to the King of Jordan saying *"if you do not shoot, we will not shoot"* but the King of Jordan succumbed to the pressure of the Islamic neighbours. He ordered his armies to battle. Fierce fighting ensued over the eastern front centering mostly on the Jerusalem areas. Two days later, Israeli paratroopers broke through the lion's gate and the city of Jerusalem was liberated.

After about 2000 years of oppression and foreign domination, the whole of Jerusalem was again in Jewish hands. No one could have done such miracles except the **Salvation/Yeshua/Jesus** of Israel Himself. This Yeshua/Jesus of Israel who is Messiah the Prince of princes, the King of kings, the Lord of lords and the God of gods, of course, stirred up the fall of Soviet Union in order to return the captivity of Israel in the late 1980s; and over half a million Jews migrated to their homeland from the Soviet bloc. Yeshua/Jesus the Messiah promised and fulfilled it!

What shall be our response to this load of information? There are similarities in Isaiah 58:12 and Isaiah 61:4. Isaiah 58:12 and 61:4 can be called the two scriptural 'witnesses' at whose mouths divine matters are established. Please, listen to the first witness in Isaiah 58:12,

- *And they that shall be of thee shall build the old waste places:*
- *thou shalt raise up the foundations of many generations;*
- *And thou shalt be called, The repairer of the breach, The restorer of the paths to dwell in.*

Then listen to the second witness in Isaiah 61:4, *And they shall build the old waste places,*

- *They shall raise up the former desolations*
- *And they shall repair the waste cities, the desolations of many generations.*

The Scriptures testify that it is not the spiritual that was first, but the natural is the first then followed by the spiritual (1Corinthians 15:46). It was first, God's natural branches or children "Israel," then, the wild branches or adopted spiritual children (the Gentiles). God temporarily placed the unbelieving natural branches under being less favoured in order to develop the spiritual branches in Yeshua/Jesus of Israel. Today, since the spiritual branches (the Gentiles) have come of age in the knowledge of ***"Yeshua/Jesus of Israel"*** God is moving to revive the natural branches across the globe by causing a great awakening. His intent is that both houses/branches would be made one new man in ***'Yeshua/Jesus of Israel'*** who alone is the Christ. By this process, we will teach principalities and powers God's manifold wisdom.

However, some of the natural Israel of God failed in their calling, thereby turning their glory into waste. They destroyed their foundations by rejecting ***"Yeshua/Jesus of Nazareth"*** the only hope of the Hebrews and the entire world. On the other hand, the spiritually engrafted children or branches (Gentiles) of God were not less in their response to their calling in ***"Yeshua/Jesus of Israel"***. They failed too and turned her cities into desolation through paganism, deification of Mary and beatification of dead saints. However, the worst that existed between the spiritual and the natural branches is ***'The Breach.'***

First, the natural branches became envious of the spiritual and the spiritual branches puffed up against the natural branches. Now let us look at Romans 11:30-31 and see the responsibility and role of the Gentiles towards Israel. *"Just as you yourselves were disobedient to God before but have received mercy now because of Israel's disobedience; so also Israel has been disobedient now, so that by your showing them the same mercy that God has shown you, they too may now receive God's mercy" (Complete Jewish Bible).* Can we say that the Gentiles have really shown the natural branches the same measure of mercy that God has shown them in helping them know the Yeshua/Jesus of Israel? Nonetheless, Paul by the Holy Ghost warned against creating dichotomy and negative responses by both houses.

SOME EVENTS IN THE DAYS OF GOD'S WRATH ON ISRAEL FROM 70AD TO 1948AD

According to history, while Israel was in exile, the few remnants and the holy land suffered several military inversions from many nations. The Romans the Islamic Turks, Greeks, Britain, etc. invaded the land of Israel. However the most painful assault on the holy land and its people was from the Roman Catholic Church. The crusaders were the military arm of the Roman Catholic Church. The Pope assigned them to go and liberate Jerusalem from the Turks, an assignment he claimed to have received from God in writing.

After the crusaders first attack on Jerusalem and their subsequent defeats in 1099AD, as the crusaders laid siege against Jerusalem, they breached the walls and conquered the city on July 15, taking it from the ruling Muslim governor. The bloodlust and cruelty of the crusaders was so great that even the battle-hardened soldiers who heard of it were appalled. Islamic men, women and children were promised clemency if they would stand under the Christian banner set on a hill after the walls were breached.

Instead of the promised clemency, those Islamic neighbours were slaughtered in their thousands by the crusaders. Seeing this, the entire Jewish community fled into their synagogue. Then the crusaders invaded them, sealed up their doors, and then set them on fire. As the inferno destroyed those Jews, those crusaders marched around the synagogue singing: *Christ we adore you.* Not a single Jew survived. Then the crusaders covered in the blood of their victims, came weeping at the tomb of Christ thanking God for their victory. However, it was surely hell rejoicing that day and not heaven because our Lord Jesus said to James and John that the Son of Man did not come to destroy the lives of men but to save them.

The Christian crusaders who claimed to be redeeming the holy land of Israel to establish the kingdom of Christ upon the earth were rather helping to destroy the kingdom and the people of Christ. This and other atrocities created ***'the breach'*** between the natural and the spiritual Israel. Israel has strong doubts on the Christian claims that we serve the same God and share the same hope. This atrocity inter-alia added to the layers of veil that covered the vision of the people of Israel concerning their Salvation/Yeshua/Jesus.

Someone might say that the crusaders were Roman Catholics and so the Protestants are exempted from this sin. History tells us that Martin Luther the father of the reformists once wrote in his book *"the Jews and their lies."* Israel as a nation has suffered too many terrible things from many nations namely wars and attempts of annihilation. The more they are threatened, the deeper the ***breach***, the more they feel isolated, and rejected.

This ***breach*** stands to stop the 'spiritual branches' from ministering to the 'natural branches' and vice versa. The prophet Isaiah prophesied that those who would receive from the ministry of ***'Yeshua/Jesus of Israel'*** the Messiah/Christ would raise former desolations, fix the breaches and repair the foundations of many generations. These factors must be touched and sorted out during this period of making the one new man in Christ.

Since wisdom is the application of knowledge or information, the following things are required from all of us:

- The church must humble themselves unto repentance and reconciliation with Israel for maltreatment and dehumanization.
- For the plunder on Israel's natural wealth during those wars, the church must make restitutions in cash and kind to Israel.
- The natural branches must also repent of the ways their fathers championed a global rejection of Yeshua/Jesus of Israel/ Nazareth as their fathers told the world that Yeshua/Jesus of Nazareth is not the true Messiah. Again, they must acknowledge the damage they have caused to heaven by telling the entire world that God the Father did not raise up the Salvation/Yeshua/Jesus of Israel from the dead as the Bible teaches.
- The natural branches must stand at the top of the mountains and tell the world that Yeshua/Jesus of Nazareth is the very 'Olive Tree' of Israel and the 'First- Born' from the dead.

If the Gentiles and Jews will apply these principles in their prayers respectively, God will begin to work wonders among the Jews and Gentiles.
This move by the Gentiles towards the Jews will definitely make Israel open their hearts to acknowledge their ***'Salvation/Yeshua/Jesus'*** who is the ***'Commonwealth'*** that connects the natural and the spiritual branches in greater measures. If in Israel's downfall, the Gentiles prospered, how much more would their restoration be! It would be life from the dead! Since 1897AD Zionism started, there have been parallel events that took place between the restoration of the natural to the spiritual restoration, and some are as follows:

- Almost in the same year, that Zionist movement gained global recognition and gathered speed that God also moved in the church. Hunger for His presence drove many Christians on their knees seeking Him. Heaven responded, and there was a phenomenal out pouring of the Spirit in the USA, Kansas, Topeka, Azusa Street between 1900–1909. In Chile, China and other recorded places across the globe witnessed a great out pour the Spirit of God.
- Almost or simultaneously, as Eliezer Ben-Yehuda restored the Hebrew language, God restored the Pentecostal tongues of fire in the church, which began to spread across the global church.
- The birth of the nation of Israel in 1948 resulted in the birth of great Christian ministries across the globe between the late 1940s and early 1950s, and

anointed men of God who helped shape the Christian world. Then some of the ministries are still alive and active today.

- June 1967 marked the end of Jerusalem's shame as the city was delivered from the hand of foreigners. Parallel to that deliverance, the Lord gifted the church with charismatic movement. The fire of God quickly spread across the Christendom breaking divisions and traditional barriers. This divine fire flowed into streams and movements, and overnight emerged charismatic Catholic, Anglican, Methodist, and Lutheran Churches, etc.
- The return of Russian Jews was parallel with the gospel spreading quickly into the same region. Massive gospel campaigns were launched and were sponsored even by the government.

If every restoration of the natural Israel had a counter spiritual reflection on the spiritual Israel, how would the restoration of Israel into the faith of our Lord Yeshua/Jesus the Christ be? It would be a kind of life from the dead! This is the hope of every committed believer waiting for the restoration of the church to her full power, glory and virtue through the knowledge of the **Salvation/Yeshua** of Israel. There have been isolated revivals here and there in recent days in the body of Christ. These revivals always happen when Israel wins a battle against their hostile neighbor's.

THE INDOMITABLE NATION OF ISRAEL THROUGH YESHUA/JESUS OF NAZARETH

From the patriarchal fathers of Israel to their offspring, the nation of Israel has been known as the 'indomitable nation.' The indomitability of the Hebrews is traced to their worshipping and serving the "***Salvation/Yeshua/Jesus of*** Israel/Nazareth who alone is the Messiah who was before Abraham and all men. Yahweh/Jehovah had promised Abraham that he would deliver his offspring from the hand of him that was stronger than his children were. *"For the LORD hath redeemed Jacob, and ransomed him from the hand of him that was stronger than he"* (Jeremiah 31:11).

The most important question we must ask ourselves is this: Since no nation was stronger than the children of Israel from the days of Abraham, Isaac and Israel, who then is this 'being' that God said that is stronger than Jacob out of whose hand Yahweh/Jehovah said He would ransom and redeem Israel? The answer to this question is found in Hosea 13:14, *"I will ransom them from the power of the grave; and I will redeem them from death: O death I will be thy plagues; O grave, I will be thy destruction: repentance shall be hid from mine eyes."*

The only being that was stronger than Abraham, Isaac, Israel and the children of Israel was the devil that had the power of death. The children of Israel seldom recorded any form of defeat in wars except in cases of idolatry and sexual sins. They were the strongest among the nations of the earth. For the sake of the Israelites and the world, Yahweh the Father *sent forth* Yahweh the Son — the **Salvation/Yeshua/Jesus of Israel/Nazareth** into the world, whom He *brought forth*. He has *sent forth* His only Son to be the *'Last Lamb'* that takes away the sin of the children of Israel and of the whole world. The Spirit of the Father granted God's Branch/Son to be sacrificed for all human beings so that through His death on the Cross of Calvary in Jerusalem, which is in the land of Moriah, He might destroy the devil that had the power of death over Adam, Abraham, Isaac, Israel and the world at large according to Hebrews 2:14.

Yahweh/Jehovah the Son—Messiah Yeshua/Jesus through His sacrificial death on mount Calvary also abolished the reign of death over Adam, Abraham, Isaac, Israel and the whole world according to 2Timothy 1:10, *"But is now made manifest by the appearing of our Saviour Jesus* Christ, who hath abolished death, and brought life and immortality to *light through the gospel."* This very high point stressed in 2Timothy 1:10, is also revealed in Romans 5:14, *"Nevertheless death reigned from Adam to Moses, even over them that had not sinned after the similitude of Adam's transgression, who is the figure of him that is to come"*

Through His death on the Cross of Calvary, Yahweh/Jehovah/the Lord Yeshua/Jesus has ransomed and redeemed His people and the world from Satan, hell, death and power of the grave. He has abolished forever the reign of death and released life and immortality to all men through the preaching of the gospel.

THE TRUE GOSPEL

The Holy Ghost made and still makes all believers in Yeshua/Jesus the Messiah/Christ who is Yahweh the Son, oracles of the gospel of Yeshua/Jesus. The greatest calling of the Jews and all Gentile believers is to be oracles of **Yeshua/Jesus of Israel.** To this end, Apostle Paul wrote to the Church in Ephesus, *"In whom ye also trusted, after that you heard the word of truth, the gospel of your* *salvation (Yeshua/Jesus): in whom also, after that ye believed, ye were sealed with that Holy Ghost of promise"* (Ephesians 1:13, Emphasis mine).

TRUE CHILDREN OF ISRAEL

The point I am about to make and stress here may appear absurd and inhumane. Nevertheless, it is the way heaven views it that I present it. Not everyone who calls himself a Jew is sealed with God's seal of the Holy Ghost. Again, it is not all who claim to be descendants of Abraham, Isaac and Israel that heaven accords recognition. The only people that God the Father recognizes as true sons of Israel are those men and women who trust and obey the gospel of **Yeshua/Jesus of Israel/Nazareth**. Such vanguards of people are the ones that the Father seals with the Holy Ghost of promise. Therefore, God does not seal Orthodox Jews with the Holy Ghost since they do not worship His Son Yeshua/Jesus of Israel. He only seals those Jews who convert from Orthodox Judaism to **Yeshua/Jesus of Nazareth** in spirit and truth. The Spirit of Yahweh/Jehovah the Father that He promised us according to Joel chapter 2 is exclusively for every Jew and Gentile who has received **Yeshua/Jesus of Israel/Nazareth** who was born in the city of David.

WARNING

All the Jews and Gentiles that worship in synagogues and other places where **Yeshua/Jesus of Israel/Nazareth** is defamed on daily basis have denied themselves the gift and sealing of the Holy Spirit. The only way by which God the Father pours out His Holy Spirit on people and seals them is, when they listen to and obey the gospel of **Yeshua/Jesus** of Nazareth our Messiah. Any Jew or Gentile who refuses the gospel of our **Yeshua/Jesus from Nazareth** does not have the Holy Ghost in him. If any Jew or Gentile who once believed that **Yeshua/Jesus** of Nazareth is the Messiah and Yahweh/Jehovah, later apostates, the Father will remove the seal of the Holy Ghost from him as He did to King Saul. Moreover, any Jew or Gentile that dies without being sealed with the Holy Ghost of promise will not enter into God's kingdom but will be cast into everlasting fire of hell.

THE PRIMARY CAUSE OF DEADLINESS AMONG THE CHURCHES IN THE WORLD

In most churches of the world today, deadliness in all phases seems to attend our church gatherings. The primary cause of this is because we have lost or cast aside the gospel of our **Yeshua/Jesus** and replaced it with the gospel of dogma. When theologies and philosophies of philosophers infiltrate churches through men on pulpits instead of the gospel of our Yeshua/Jesus, God seals no one with the Holy Ghost of promise. Evidently, it was when Apostle Peter preached the unadulterated gospel of our **Yeshua/Jesus** to the house of Cornelius that God the Father poured out His Holy Spirit of promise on them and then sealed them for His kingdom. The family of Cornelius became the first Gentile family to be blessed with Joel 2 and to be sealed with the Holy Ghost.

If Peter had preached the gospel of the Pharisees to Brother Cornelius and his household (heaven forbid), God would not have poured out His Spirit on them and no one would have been sealed. In Roman Catholic Church, for example, where their popes and reverend fathers preach the gospel of Mary and worshipping of molded images instead of presenting *the gospel of our Yeshua/Jesus of Nazareth* to the people, God the Father withholds the outpour of His Spirit from them.

In addition, because of this reason given above, no one is sealed with the Holy Spirit of promise who alone is the only source of power to the church. The unadulterated study, belief, preaching, teaching and preservation of the '*glorious gospel*' of our Yahweh/Jehovah the Son— Jesus Christ of Nazareth/Israel is the only way our heavenly Father is invited to our earthly gatherings. In Anglican, Methodist, Presbyterian, and all the Pentecostal churches where the doctrines and constitutions of men are preached instead of the '*glorious gospel*' of our Yeshua/Jesus, there abides abject deadliness.

When we live our lives based on the '*glorious gospel*' of our Lord Jesus Christ only, His Father rewards us by pouring out the Holy Ghost of promise upon us and seals us therewith until the redemption of the purchased possession. It is only through the means of the '*pure and glorious gospel*' of our Lord Jesus preached and taught in churches, synagogues, private places, business forums and centres, marriages and governmental platforms by His true friends that deadliness can be eliminated and swept away from us completely.

The gospel or 'Good News' of our **Salvation/Yeshua/Jesus** is also called the '*Word of Truth.*' Our primary assignment as believing Jews and Gentiles in the Salvation/Yeshua/Jesus of Israel/Nazareth is to study, believe and teach others the gospel of our **Salvation/Yeshua** as Apostle Paul and others did. The gospel is this:

Yeshua/Jesus of Israel/Nazareth is both our Messiah and Yahweh/Jehovah to the glory of God the Father, world without end.

Oh, Citizens Of Israel Apparently Living In The Land Of Israel And Those In Diaspora Know That Yeshua/Jesus Of Israel/ Nazareth Is Our Only And True Messiah. "And as many as walk according to this rule, peace be on them, and mercy, and upon the Israel of God" (Galatians 6:16).

SELECTED BIBLIOGRAPHY

1. The Name of Jesus in the Old Testament by Arthur E. Glass
2. Exposition on the Aleph—Bet by Rabbi Michael L. Munk of the New York in his 'The Wisdom in the Hebrew Alphabet'
3. Roman Catholic Misuse of Genesis 3:15 by Keith Thompson
4. Who is this Allah? By G.J.O. Moshay
5. Streams of blood by Elder Nathaniel Ndukwe
6. Jehovah's Witnesses EXPOSED

CONTACTS:

+234-803-097-7534

+234-812-576-4801
+234-803-292-3386

ISBN 978-978-52584 9-3

www.ingramcontent.com/pod-product-compliance
Lightning Source LLC
Chambersburg PA
CBHW080518090426
42734CB00015B/3093

* 9 7 8 9 7 8 5 2 5 8 4 9 3 *